T0358213

Cambridge Elements ☰

Elements in International Relations
edited by
Jon C. W. Pevehouse
University of Wisconsin–Madison
Tanja A. Börzel
Freie Universität Berlin
Edward D. Mansfield
University of Pennsylvania
Associate Editors-International Security
Sarah Kreps
Cornell University
Anna Leander
Graduate Institute Geneva

AFTER HEDGING

Hard Choices for the Indo-Pacific States Between the United States and China

Kai He
Griffith University

Huiyun Feng
Griffith University

CAMBRIDGE
UNIVERSITY PRESS

Shaftesbury Road, Cambridge CB2 8EA, United Kingdom

One Liberty Plaza, 20th Floor, New York, NY 10006, USA

477 Williamstown Road, Port Melbourne, VIC 3207, Australia

314–321, 3rd Floor, Plot 3, Splendor Forum, Jasola District Centre,
New Delhi – 110025, India

103 Penang Road, #05–06/07, Visioncrest Commercial, Singapore 238467

Cambridge University Press is part of Cambridge University Press & Assessment,
a department of the University of Cambridge.

We share the University's mission to contribute to society through the pursuit of
education, learning and research at the highest international levels of excellence.

www.cambridge.org
Information on this title: www.cambridge.org/9781009462693

DOI: 10.1017/9781009420570

First published 2023

A catalogue record for this publication is available from the British Library

ISBN 978-1-009-46269-3 Hardback
ISBN 978-1-009-42058-7 Paperback
ISSN 2515-706X (online)
ISSN 2515-7302 (print)

After Hedging

Hard Choices for the Indo-Pacific States Between the United States and China

Elements in International Relations

DOI: 10.1017/9781009420570
First published online: September 2023

Kai He
Griffith University

Huiyun Feng
Griffith University

Author for correspondence: Kai He, k.he@griffith.edu.au, hekai@yahoo.com

Abstract: The strategic rivalry between the United States and China has heightened since COVID-19. Secondary states face increasing difficulties maintaining a "hedging" strategy between the United States and China. This Element introduces a preference-for-change model to explain the policy variations of states during the order transition. It suggests that policymakers will perceive a potential change in the international order through a cost–benefit prism. The interplays between the perceived costs and the perception of benefits from the order transition will shape states' policy choices among four strategic options: (1) hedging to bet on uncertainties; (2) bandwagoning with rising powers to support changes; (3) balancing against rising powers to resist changes; and (4) buck-passing to ignore changes. Four case studies (Australia, New Zealand, Singapore, and Thailand) are conducted to explore the policy choices of regional powers during the international order transition. This title is also available as Open Access on Cambridge Core.

Keywords: Indo Pacific, US–China Strategic Competition, Hedging, Balancing, Bandwagoning, Buck-Passing

ISBNs: 9781009462693 (HB), 9781009420587 (PB), 9781009420570 (OC)
ISSNs: 2515-706X (online), 2515-7302 (print)

Contents

Introduction

The strategic rivalry between the United States and China has intensified since the COVID-19 pandemic, which has accelerated the potential international order transition, as noted by Kissinger (2020) and Haass (2020). The constant downward spiral of US–China relations might eventually push the two countries into a corner – a new Cold War or even the "Thucydides trap" – a military conflict between the hegemon and a rising power (Allison, 2017; Feng & He, 2020; Kynge, Manson, & Politi, 2020). Some scholars suggest that a new Cold War is on the doorstep if the United States decouples from China (e.g., Rachman, 2020), while others argue that strategic competition without ideological antagonism will not lead to a new Cold War (e.g., Christensen, 2021).

It is still unclear whether a new Cold War between the United States and China is coming. However, China has been seen as "America's most consequential geopolitical challenge" in the latest Biden-Harris administration's National Security Strategy despite the ongoing Ukraine War in Europe. It is simply because China is "the only competitor with both the intent to reshape the international order and, increasingly, the economic, diplomatic, military, and technological power to do it" (White House, 2022a). The first face-to-face meeting between Biden and Xi since Biden became president during the G20 summit in November 2022 seemed to offer some hope of repairing the damaged bilateral relations between the two great powers. However, since the "balloon incident" in February 2023, the strategic competition between the United States and China has escalated.

In March 2023, President Xi publicly accused the United States of attempting to contain, encircle, and suppress China (Bradsher, 2023). Additionally, the meeting between Taiwan's President Tsai and US Speaker of the House Kevin McCarthy in Los Angeles in April 2023 has further strained the already contentious bilateral relationship. As of June 2023, when this Element was written, it was reported that China persisted in rejecting the Pentagon's request for a defense minister meeting at the Shangri-La Dialogue in Singapore. As Biden clearly states, the United States will "compete vigorously with the PRC" but "the competition should not veer into conflict" (White House, 2022b). It is clear that the two states will engage in intense competition with one another through multiple means, including international institutions, in the foreseeable future.

Differing from Trump's unilateralist approach, the Biden administration has been working on building a "grand alliance" against China since 2021 (Lee, 2021; Macias, 2021). Although both the feasibility and effectiveness of such an anti-China alliance are questionable during the order transition, other states in the region, such as Australia, Japan, and the ASEAN states, are facing strategic pressures from the United States as well as from China. In other words, sooner or later the structural imperative during the potential order transition will force them to make a policy choice between the two giants.[1] Since 2008, we have witnessed various policy choices by secondary powers beyond hedging in the region. For example, Australia seems to have chosen a balancing strategy by strengthening its "mateship" with the United States against China's challenge to the rules-based order. Even among the Five-Eye countries, New Zealand's policy toward China seems to have departed from others, especially on whether to upgrade this intelligence-sharing organization to an anti-China diplomatic grouping (Dziedzic, 2021). At the same time, we also notice that Singapore's Prime Minister Lee Hsien Loong has reiterated that it is not in the interest of Singapore and other Asian countries to pick sides between the United States and China (Lee Hsien Loong, 2020). Why and how do states choose different foreign policies during the international order transition? These are important, but somehow less studied, questions in the field of foreign policy analysis. Secondary powers' policy choices will not only influence the power dynamics between the United States and China but also shape the regional security architecture and potential order transition in the international system.

It is worth noting that in IR (international relations) theory, different schools of thought have different conceptualizations of the international order (He & Feng, 2020). In a realist world, as Joseph Nye Jr. points out, the so-called international order equals the international system, which is defined by material power capabilities among states (Nye, 2003, p. 254). John Mearsheimer suggests that international order is "an organized group of international institutions that help govern interactions among member states . . . great powers create and manage orders" (Mearsheimer, 2019, p. 9). Similarly, Charles Glaser points out that "an international order should be understood as a means, not an end. A state or states create an order to achieve certain ends. Similarly, a state can choose to join an order – abide by its rules and norms and participate in its institutions – in pursuit of its interests (i.e., ends)" (Glaser, 2019, p. 57). Although international institutions and rules are highlighted, they are normally treated as diplomatic tools for states to pursue their power-based interests. Therefore, institutions are epiphenomenal in world politics and what really matters is power, according to Mearsheimer (1994/1995).

Liberalism, constructivism, and the English School challenge this power-based realist understanding of international order although they hold diverse views on the role of institutions, rules, and norms in an international order. For liberals, an international order is manifested by the functions of rules and

---

[1] There is a third policy choice, which is to stay away from the US–China competition. We treat this policy as "buck-passing" and will discuss it in Section 5.

institutions. For example, G. John Ikenberry suggests that "International order refers to the organizing rules and institutions of world politics. It is the governing arrangements that define and guide the relations among states" (Ikenberry, 2017, p. 59). Here, Ikenberry highlights the functional role of rules and institutions, which facilitates the creation of a "functioning political system" among states. Differing from realists like Mearsheimer who suggest institutions, rules, and even the order itself are just instruments or means for states to maximize interests, liberals argue that these rules and institutions embedded in the order have an independent function in governing interstate relationships. It is why Ikenberry famously contends that US hegemony might decline, but the liberal international order (LIO) will sustain. More importantly, China's rise does not mean the end of the LIO (Ikenberry, 2008, 2018).

For constructivists and the English School scholars, norms, ideas, and values are constitutive parts of an international order. As Jeffrey Legro points out, "international order is made by national ideas, so is it unmade" (Legro, 2005, p. 1). Muthiah Alagappa defines international order as "a formal or informal arrangement that sustains rule-governed interaction among sovereign states in their pursuit of individual and collective goals" (Alagappa, 2003, p. 39). Hedley Bull conceptualized international order as "a pattern of activity that sustains the elementary or primary goals of the society of states, or international society" (Bull, 1977, p. 8). In defining international order, we can see how constructivism and the English School emphasize the constitutive role of ideas, values, and goals in making an international order. The functional perspective of liberalism on institutions and order is rooted in the consequential logic of rationalism; constructivism and the English School, to a different extent, follow the logic of appropriateness with a strong normative element in their conceptualization of international order.

Similarly, scholars hold different views on the potential order transition and the future of US hegemony. Some suggest that the liberal international order will survive despite crises and challenges (Lake, Martin, & Risse, 2021), while others argue that the order transition is taking place because the liberal international order is doomed (Glaser, 2019; Mearsheimer, 2019). Here, we take a middle-ground position to define both international order and international order transition. International order is conceptualized as "a normative and institutional arrangement among sovereign states that governs their interactions in the power-based international system." This definition of international order integrates the three pillars of international order: norms, institutions, and power from constructivism (including the English School), liberalism, and realism respectively (He & Feng, 2020, p. 12, 2023). In addition, we define "international order transition" as "a changing process of the normative, institutional, and power foundations of the current international order." We suggest that China's rise has triggered a process of international order transition in the Asia Pacific, not in the world, because it has not challenged all three pillars of the current international order. The final outcome of the current international order, that is, the US-led liberal international order, is still uncertain (He & Feng, 2023).[2]

This project examines different foreign policy choices adopted by regional powers in the context of US–China strategic competition against the background of the potential international order transition. It introduces a "preference-for-change" model – a neoclassical realist argument – to explain how different perceptions of political leaders regarding the system-level order transition shape their policy choices toward the United States and China. It suggests that policy-makers will perceive potential change of the international order through a cost–benefit prism.[3] The interplay between the perceived costs and the perceived benefits from the international order transition shall shape states' policy choices among four strategic options: (1) hedging to bet on uncertainties regarding change; (2) bandwagoning with rising powers to support change; (3) balancing against rising powers to resist change; and (4) buck-passing to ignore change.

There are four sections in the project. First, we discuss the existent literature on states' policy choices during international order transition. We argue that most research focuses on the two giants but pays limited attention to the diverse behavior of other players during an order transition. Second, we introduce our neoclassical realist model – a "preference-for-change" argument – to illustrate how policymakers' perceptions of order transition shape different policy choices of states toward the United States and China. Third, we conduct four short case studies to test our model by examining the foreign policy orientations of Australia, Singapore, Thailand, and New Zealand during the ongoing order transition featuring the US–China strategic competition. In conclusion, we argue that although the international order transition is inevitable, the United States and China can make a difference on how the change will take place. A peaceful change in the international order is not impossible, but it will need to be largely determined by wise policy choices from both the United States and China.

---

[2] For other examples of different views on the liberal international order, see Ikenberry (2018); Paul (2021).

[3] Although our model highlights leaders' cost–benefit perceptions in shaping a state's policy choice, it does not deny the importance of other domestic and ideational variables in complex decision-making processes. Nor does it deny possible domestic contestations of different leaders' perceptions regarding the international order transition. However, our model adopts a rational choice approach, following epistemological parsimony. For parsimony versus accuracy, see Almond & Genco (1977).

1 International Order Transition and State Policy Choice

Explaining change is an enduring but tough task in world politics (Gilpin, 1981; Paul, 2017, 2018; He & Chan, 2018). International order transition is one of the major changes in world politics. How states behave during the dynamic period of order transition will, to a certain extent, shape the nature and outcome of the order transition, that is, whether it will be violent or peaceful. Existing research has three limitations in the study of state policy choices during the order transition: the great power bias toward balancing, the lack of dynamics for hedging, and the eroding role of institutions for secondary powers.

Realism, especially power transition theory, has paid close attention to international order transition and equated the change of power distribution in the international system to international order transition (Organski, 1958; Organski & Kugler, 1980; Nye, 2003; Chan et al., 2021). Therefore, their focus is mainly on great powers, especially the declining hegemon and rising powers. For example, Graham Allison has warned about the danger of Thucydides's Trap, in which there will be a direct military clash between the United States and China during international order transition (Allison, 2017). For realism, hard balancing, including military build-up (internal balancing) and alliance formation (external balancing), is the main policy choice for both rising great powers and the declining hegemon (Waltz, 1979; Mearsheimer, 2001). Although recent IR scholarship stretches the concept of balancing to include nonmilitary "soft balancing" behaviors, the essence of "soft balancing" is to prepare for "hard balancing" in the future (Pape, 2005; Paul, 2005; He & Feng, 2008).

Under the Obama administration, the United States launched its "pivot" or "rebalance" toward Asia by strengthening its military cooperation with traditional allies and security partners, especially after the 2008 global financial crisis. Trump's trade war against China starting in 2018 and the Free and Open Indo-Pacific Strategy (FOIP) by the US government were a manifestation of the intense strategic competition between the two nations. After Biden assumed power, the US security policy toward the region largely followed Trump's FOIP footsteps, although Biden highlighted the importance of alliances and multilateralism in dealing with China's challenges. For Chinese leaders, Obama's "pivot toward Asia," Trump's "trade war," and Biden's multilateral approach all represent a clear sign of balancing, including both hard balancing and soft balancing with a containment purpose against China (Lieberthal & Wang, 2012; Liu, 2023). Apparently, balancing, especially hard balancing with military means, is the major game between the United States and China during the order transition. However, the problem for realism in general and power transition theory in particular is that they fail to explain the diverse behavior of other states during the order transition.

As mentioned in the Introduction, while Australia seemed to choose a balancing policy by strengthening its "mateship" with the United States against China's challenge to the rules-based order, other traditional allies of the United States, such as South Korea, Japan, Thailand, and the Philippines, have tried to walk a thin line between the United States and China through an accommodation and even bandwagoning strategy (Kang, 2003; Ross, 2006). In addition, other non-US allies, such as Cambodia and Laos, have strengthened their bilateral relationships with China against the United States. It is clear that neither balancing nor bandwagoning can capture the variations of states' policy choices in the context of US–China competition during the period of order transition.

To address this "great power bias," some scholars advocate a hedging argument in explaining the ambiguous behaviors of secondary states amidst the strategic rivalry between the United States and China. Hedging is a term from the finance and business world. It refers to a form of investment insurance aiming to reduce investment risk. Typically, hedging involves investing in two securities with a negative correlation. It means that if one security loses value, the other gains value. In the IR and security studies literatures, hedging refers to a policy involving both cooperative and competitive elements (Art, 2004). Some scholars further define hedging as a middle-position policy between balancing and bandwagoning in an academic sense or between cooperation and containment in policy terminology (Medeiros, 2005; Foot, 2006; Goh, 2006; Kang, 2007; Kuik, 2008).[4]

For example, Cheng-Chwee Kuik defines hedging as one of alignment behaviors by states with "ambiguous, mixed and 'opposite' positioning" in policy orientation (Kuik, 2016, p. 502; also Kuik, 2008). Empirically, he suggests that:

> over the past two decades – amidst the power reconfigurations in the Asia–Pacific following the end of the Cold War circa 1990 and the onset of the global economic crisis in 2008 – the small and medium-sized Southeast Asian states have all pursued a mixed and opposite strategy [hedging] towards the re-emerging China (Kuik, 2016, p. 503).

Ikenberry groups secondary powers as "middle states" between the United States and China, arguing that "short of these grand alternatives, middle states appear to be pursuing more mixed strategies of engagement and hedging" (Ikenberry, 2016, p. 28). Here, while engagement means to develop economic

---

[4] For other definitions and applications of hedging, see Park (2011); Tessman & Wolfe (2011); Tessman (2012); Jackson (2014); Ciorciari (2019); Ciorciari & Haacke (2019); Foot & Goh (2019); Haacke (2019); Liff (2019); Lim & Mukherjee (2019); Korolev (2019); Jones & Jenne (2021).

relations with China, hedging in Ikenberry's terms refers to a strategy of these states to "deepen security ties to the United States" (Ikenberry, 2016, p. 29).

Despite the nuanced differences in conceptualizing "hedging," most scholars agree that hedging is a prevailing policy choice located between hard balancing and bandwagoning.[5] Hedging indeed captures the mixed nature of policy choices for states, especially secondary powers, between cooperation and confrontation when the international order is relatively stable under unipolarity. The structural stability in the post–Cold War unipolar world has reduced the strategic antagonism in the system and created a rare condition in which secondary states can enjoy the freedom of action to engage and cooperate with both the United States and China (Wohlforth, 1999; Ayson, 2012). To a certain extent, not only did secondary states choose to hedge, but the United States and China have also conducted "mutual hedging" against each other with both cooperative and confrontational elements in their policy choices in the post–Cold War era (Medeiros, 2005).

However, the hedging scholarship faces an analytical problem – a lack of dynamics – during the period of international order transition. The international order is changing, and so is a state's hedging strategy. The changing international order and the intensifying power competition between great powers have made it difficult, if not impossible, for secondary powers to keep their hedging strategies. It has become a political cliché for leaders of secondary states to publicly claim that it is not in their countries' interests to pick sides between the United States and China. From the perspective of secondary states, hedging is certainly a preferred strategy because it can maximize both security and economic interests. Therefore, some states, like Singapore, might still decide to actively engage in a hedging strategy between the United States and China despite the systemic pressures from the two giants. However, the increasing strategic competition between the United States and China will somehow force these secondary states to make a strategic choice, sooner or later, between the United States and China although *when* these states will give up the hedging option is still a debatable question. Different countries might have various "tipping points" in their decision-making processes, but a general trend is that secondary states will have to make a decision beyond hedging at a certain point during the period of order transition.[6]

For example, Australia has formed a new security deal – AUKUS – with the United States and the United Kingdom in September 2021. It is widely seen as

---

[5] Some classical realists, however, suggest that hedging is not an intentional strategy by second-tier states. Instead, it is "a counsel of prudence in the conduct of statecraft that fits strategic ends to limited means." See Jones & Jenne (2021, p. 3).

[6] The authors thank Rosemary Foot for raising this "tipping point" issue in discussing when states might change a hedging strategy during the order transition.

the end of Australia's decades-long hedging between the United States and China (Westcott, 2021). It is not to suggest that it is impossible to keep a hedging strategy between the United States and China. However, hedging has lost its prime time as a preferable policy choice for secondary states in the period of international order transition. The unaddressed questions for hedging scholars, therefore, are under what condition and why do some states change their hedging strategy while others do not amidst the international order transition? Although we do not deny that secondary states might prefer hedging or choose hedging as long as they can, one critical question is: what will secondary states do if they can no longer hedge between the United States and China?

Besides hard balancing and hedging, some scholars argue that the ideas, rules, and norms of international institutions can facilitate the efforts of secondary states to constrain and even shape great powers' behaviors. For example, Kai He suggests that the ASEAN states employed an institutional balancing strategy to constrain China's behavior through the ASEAN Regional Forum (ARF) in the 1990s (He, 2008, 2009). Evelyn Goh argues that after the Cold War, the ASEAN states successfully applied an enmeshment strategy to socialize China's foreign policy behavior through ASEAN-oriented multilateralism (Goh, 2007). Similarly, Alastair Iain Johnston suggests that Chinese policymakers were socialized by ASEAN's cooperative security norms through participating in ASEAN-oriented institutions, such as the ARF, in the post–Cold War era (Johnston, 2014). The proliferation of multilateral institutions and the well-established "ASEAN centrality" in regional affairs vindicate the importance of international institutions in international relations of the Asia Pacific.

However, this institution-based argument has an analytical weakness in explaining secondary states' policy choices in the period of order transition. The intensifying strategic tension between the United States and China has squeezed the strategic space of secondary powers in international affairs, including their previous role in multilateralism. As mentioned earlier, ASEAN played an active and even leading role in constructing multilateralism in the Asia Pacific in the post–Cold War era. However, this independent role of ASEAN in constraining and shaping great power behaviors has been eroding in recent years because both China and the United States have started to dominate the institutional games through their preferred and initiated multilateral institutions (He, 2019, 2020).

For example, China initiated the Belt and Road Initiative (BRI), which is seen as its economic hub-and-spokes system in the region (Cha, 2018; Gong, 2019; Rolland, 2019; Pal & Singh, 2020). In addition, China started to play a leadership role in building China-centered security and economic institutions, such as the revival of CICA (Conference on Interaction and Confidence

Building in Asia) in regional security and AIIB (Asian Infrastructure Investment Bank) in infrastructure finance. In a similar vein, the United States under the Obama administration used TPP (Trans-Pacific Partnership) to build an exclusive trading block against China. The FOIP (Free and Open Indo-Pacific) strategy started by the Trump administration has been extended by President Biden in that the Quadrilateral Security Dialogue (the Quad) among the United States, Japan, India, and Australia is becoming a new institutional balancing tool targeting China. Moreover, in May 2022, the Biden administration launched a new multilateral economic initiative – the Indo-Pacific Economic Framework (IPEF) – with twelve countries in the region, aiming at "writing the new rules for the 21st-century economy" (Biden, 2022). China was not invited to join the IPEF, which is widely seen as an economic arm of the US FOIP strategy balancing against China's economic power and influence in the region. In these new institutions led by China and the United States, the relevance of ASEAN in particular and secondary powers in general has been limited, although both China and the United States still publicly endorse the "ASEAN centrality." To a certain extent, these second-tier states face a similar dilemma in having to choose between the United States and China among as well as inside these new multilateral institutions.

In sum, realism, especially power transition theory, focuses on the military and security aspect of state behavior, while the hedging school seems to highlight the mixed elements of economic cooperation and security competition in a state's policy choices. Institutionalists from both rationalism and constructivism (including the English School) emphasize the role of institutions and norms in enriching the repertoire of a state's policy strategy. One unaddressed limitation, however, is that the existing research fails to fully account for the dynamic nature of a state's foreign policy options during the period of order transition.

2 Preference-for-Change Model: A Neoclassical Realist Framework

In this project we propose a "preference-for-change" argument – a neoclassical realist framework – to shed some light on various policy behaviors of states during the period of order transition (Rose, 1998; Rathbun, 2008; Lobell, Ripsman, & Taliaferro, 2009; Ripsman, Taliaferro, & Lobell, 2016). Neoclassical realism is not a single theory, but a research program or theoretical framework rooted in the realist research tradition of studies on foreign policy and international politics. According to Ripsman, Taliaferro, and Lobell (2016), there are three types of neoclassical realism.[7] Type I neoclassical realists, as identified by Gideon Rose in his review essay, which coins the term "neoclassical realism," mainly focus on addressing the anomaly cases that structural realism cannot explain well. For example, Randall Schweller (1998) introduces a balance-of-interests argument to explain why states failed to balance against Hitler's aggression before the Second World War by examining different types or natures of states in the international system. Other Type I neoclassical realist works include Stephen Walt's balance of threat theory (1987), Thomas Christensen's political mobilization model (1996), and J. W. Taliaferro's balance of risk theory (2004).

As Gideon Rose observes, the reason for grouping these different theories together is that neoclassical realists share a similar theoretical framework that differentiates them from classical realists and structural realists. Simply put, if we see classical realism as "first image" (individual level) and structural realism as "third image" (system level) approaches, neoclassical realism is a multilevel approach, whose research framework crosses individual (first image), domestic (second image), and systemic (third image) levels of analysis (Lobell, Ripsman, & Taliaferro, 2009; He, 2016). All these Type I neoclassical realists start their research by identifying the historical anomalies that structural realism, especially Waltz's neorealism, cannot explain. Then they introduce some intervening variables from the domestic level and draw new causal mechanisms between systemic effects and state behaviors to fix the problem of structural realism in explaining states' foreign policies. Neoclassical realists borrow explanatory power from both structural realism and classical realism because "the systemic pressures must be translated through intervening variables at the unit level" (Rose, 1998, pp. 145–46).

Type II neoclassical realism follows the footstep of Type I neoclassical realists by further theorizing neoclassical realist frameworks in explaining state behavior. Some exemplary works are included in the edited volume by Lobell, Ripsman and Taliaferro (2009). Type II neoclassical realists do not necessarily start their research with an empirical puzzle that structural realists cannot explain. Instead, they focus on systemic stimuli, moderated by domestic-level intervening variables, to develop a more general foreign policy approach according to the realist research tradition. To a certain extent, the rise of Type II neoclassical realism is a theoretical response to the old debate among realists over whether structural realism can explain a state's foreign policy (Elman, 1996; Waltz, 1996). Methodologically and epistemologically, Type II neoclassical realism does not have any differences from Type I. The major difference between Type I and Type II neoclassical realists is that most Type I scholars are passively labeled as neoclassical realists by their

---

[7] Here we focus on the soft positivist approach in neoclassical realism while acknowledging that there are more critical and reflective variants of neoclassical realist works. See Meibauer et al. (2021).

works, while Type II scholars are more consciously applying the neoclassical realist framework and intentionally enriching the research program by further theorizing various intervening variables in their research.

In their 2016 book, Ripsman, Taliaferro, and Lobell develop an ambitious Type III research program of neoclassical realism. The most significant difference between Type I and Type II on the one hand and Type III on the other is the dependent variable in their research. While the former types focus on foreign policy choices, the latter expands to international politics – the interactions or outcomes of state behaviors. Moreover, Ripsman, Taliaferro, and Lobell (2016, pp. 12–13) identify four broad classes of intervening variables, including leader images, strategic culture, domestic institutions, and state–society relations, as well as three intervening-level processes between systemic effects and state behaviors, including perceptions of the international system, decision making, and resource mobilization or policy implementation. While Type III neoclassical realists' intellectual efforts in further theorizing intervening variables for neoclassical realism are highly admirable, their ambition to make neoclassical realism a grand theory of international politics is questionable and debatable (Narizny, 2017; Smith, 2018).

As a midrange theoretical framework from the realism tradition, Type I and Type II neoclassical realism can enjoy some intellectual freedom to develop better empirical explanations by focusing on various domestic-intervening variables and innovative causal mechanisms. Although some scholars have criticized this neoclassical realist approach as the paradigmatic degeneration of realism (Legro & Moravcsik, 1999; Tang, 2009; Narizny, 2017), a typical neoclassical realist response is that solving empirical puzzles is more important than keeping paradigmatic purity (Schweller, 2003; Rathbun, 2008). More importantly, Type I and Type II neoclassical realists follow the eclectic approach to borrow insights from other theoretical paradigms, such as liberalism and constructivism, to enrich our understanding of foreign policy choices of states in the anarchic international system (Sil & Katzenstein, 2010).

In comparison, the Type III neoclassical realists attempt to systemize the approach and develop a grand IR theory to examine the interactive outcomes of states' foreign policies. One potential challenge, however, is that the causal linkage between states' foreign policies and international outcomes is unclear. The aggregation of individual states' behaviors might or might not directly link to the outcomes of international politics. For example, if all states conduct internal balancing by strengthening their military capabilities, it will trigger arms races among states. However, arms races among states might not lead to system-level conflict or war because states might keep the system-level balance of power, which reduces the possibility of conflict in the system. In other words, if we treat the international system as a complex adaptive system (Jervis, 1998), how to capture system effects based on individual state behaviors will be a potential challenge for Type III neoclassical realists in the future.

In this research, we follow the Type I and II approaches of neoclassical realism to explain states' different foreign policy choices under systemic constraints of potential order transition between the United States and China in the international system. In conclusion, we shall adopt the Type III neoclassical realist approach to preliminarily discuss the potential implications of our findings for international order transition. Still, our preference-for-change model is a Type I/II neoclassical realist argument, mainly focused on explaining states' foreign policy choices. We, however, encourage other scholars, including Type III neoclassical realists, to further examine the systemic outcomes of these states' foreign policy choices based on our findings.

Our preference-for-change model argues that the changing dynamics of the international system in the form of order transition is the main reason for states to choose diverse policy choices. However, this systemic effect on foreign policy behavior is transmitted through leaders' perceptions regarding the cost–benefit calculation of the ongoing order transition. In other words, political leaders' cost–benefit-based preference for change of the international order transition shall shape a state's policy choice during the period of order transition. The independent variable of the "preference-for-change" model is the changing dynamics of the international order. Two intervening variables of the model are political leaders' perceptions regarding the costs and benefits of the ongoing order transition. Both perceptions are measured as high and low. The interplay of the cost and benefit perceptions regarding the potential order transition, reflecting policymakers' preferences for change, shall shape the variations of the model's dependent variable – foreign policy choices. The causal mechanism between order transition in the international system and policy choices of states is the cost–benefit perceptions of political leaders regarding the order transition. Cognitively, political leaders' perceptions play an important role in shaping their policy behaviors although other factors might also influence a state's policy decisions (Levy, 2013; Stein, 2013).

Building on existing research, we have listed four types of state policy choices during the order transition: balancing, bandwagoning, hedging, and buck-passing. As mentioned before, these policy behaviors are closely associated with certain schools of thought in the IR literature as well as with a focus on issue areas. For example, balancing and bandwagoning are seen as opposite to military alliance behavior by realists (Waltz, 1979; Walt, 1987). Buck-passing is also treated as passive behavior in the security alignment literature (Christensen & Schneider, 1990). Hedging seems to blend both economic cooperation and security competition from liberalism and realism. It is worth noting that hedging is still a valid policy choice in our model although we argue that it will become more and more difficult for secondary states to sustain given the structural pressures from US–China competition.

Here we follow the "soft balancing" tradition to relax the traditional issue-based and paradigm-latent definitions of these four foreign policy behaviors (Pape, 2005; Paul, 2005; He & Feng, 2008). It means that balancing does not specifically refer to a "military" alignment strategy. Instead, it indicates a general alignment orientation of a state's foreign policy in different issue areas. In other words, states can choose different types of balancing, such as hard balancing, soft balancing, and institutional balancing, to pursue power and influence in the international system.

We argue that all four foreign policy behaviors – balancing, bandwagoning, hedging, and buck-passing – aim at increasing a state's security, power, influence, and status in world politics, which can be broadly defined as a state's interests according to structural realism. It is worth noting that neoclassical realism is rooted in structural realism, especially neorealism, which highlights the constraining effects of anarchy on states in the international system.[8] According to Kenneth Waltz (1979, p. 126), "In anarchy, security is the highest end. Only if survival is assured can states safely seek such other goals as tranquility, profit, and power." Therefore, we do not deny that states have different interests. However, our analysis highlights the security imperative for states derived from anarchy in the international system. These four policy choices, balancing, bandwagoning, buck-passing, and hedging, can be seen as a state's policy alignment orientation versus others to pursue security and other related interests (after ensuring survival) in the anarchic international system. Again, policy alignment does not only refer to military alliance. Instead, it means a general policy option of a state toward others in different issue areas under anarchy. For example, a state can form an institutional alignment with others so that they can cooperate within an institutional setting. A state can also forge a political alignment with others with similar political goals. In practice, G7 could be seen as an economic, institutional, as well as political alignment among advanced economies sharing a similar democratic system in the world.

Table 1 summarizes the conceptual and operational differences among these four state policy choices during an order transition. Here, following Randall

---

[8] How to define a state's national interests is a debatable question for different stripes of realists. For example, classical realists, like Hans Morgenthau, define national interests in terms of power. While both defensive and offensive realists believe that security is the highest end for states under anarchy, they differ in how to pursue security. The former advocate a self-constrained strategy, while the latter, like Mearsheimer, believe that the best way to pursue security is to maximize power and achieve regional hegemony. See Morgenthau (1967); Glaser (1997, 2010); Mearsheimer (2001). For different stripes of realism, see Wohlforth (2008).

Table 1 A typological explanation of state policy choices during international order transition

	Threat perception	Benefit expectation	Behavioral preference	Policy Goal
Balancing	High-level threat	Low to no expectation of benefit	Form alliances to counter threat from rising powers	Minimize potential risks
Bandwagoning	Lowest-level threat	High expectation of benefit	Work closely with rising powers for profits	Maximize potential benefits
Hedging	Medium-level or uncertain	Uncertain	Cautiously engage both incumbent and rising powers	Neutralize or offset potential risks
Buck-passing	Low-level threat or not an urgent threat	High expectation of benefit	Stay away from the competition and do business as usual	Avoid potential risks

Schweller's definition of balancing and bandwagoning, we define balancing as a state's policy alignment strategy "driven by the desire to avoid losses," where the immediate purpose of balancing is to self-preserve and protect the values that a state already possesses (Schweller, 1994, p. 74). Similarly, bandwagoning is a state's policy alignment strategy that is "driven by the opportunity for gain." The immediate purpose of bandwagoning is to "obtain values coveted" (Schweller, 1994, p. 74). In practice, two states are more likely to form a military alliance against a common threat because the alliance can help them to avoid losses and protect their security and sovereignty just as Walt's balance of threat theory suggests (Walt, 1987). However, as Schweller points out, many states have joined military alliances – a military form of alignments – not because they were facing common threats, but due to their perceived "rewards and profits" (Schweller, 1994). Again, we use Schweller's re-conceptualization of balancing versus bandwagoning, but we relax the usage of the term beyond the military domain.

For hedging, we suggest that it is a state's alignment policy aiming to offset risks so that the state can manage well the perceived gains and losses. Again, hedging is a policy choice beyond the traditional military and security domain. It can be applied in economic, political, and institutional arenas or as a mixed strategy to use economic gains to offset potential security losses or vice versa. As for buck-passing, strictly speaking it is not an alignment policy per se. Instead, it is a policy to avoid risk-latent alignment. It is worth noting that without a limited alignment, a state will not be able to pass "bucks" or risks to others. However, the limited alignment under buck-passing is not to countervail potential threats. Instead, it is a preparation for transferring risks or passing "bucks" in the future. Here, buck-passing is defined as a policy strategy to avoid possible risks from certain or potential change in the international system. Compared to hedging in terms of actively offsetting risks, buck-passing is more passive in nature. Moreover, a buck-passing strategy means to intentionally stay away from potential conflicts among great powers caused by the order transition.

As mentioned before, the perceptions of change regarding the associated costs and benefits during order transition are coded as high and low. As shown in Figure 1, the interplays between the two variables (the cost perception and the benefit perception) shape the different policy choices of states during the order transition.

Cell 1 in Figure 1 indicates a situation where both the cost and benefit perceptions of international order transitions are high. It means that a state's policymakers are highly uncertain about the future international order. On the one hand, they can see the potential economic and security benefits from the order transition because the rising power challenging the existing order might provide more public and private goods to others in the future international order. On the other hand, they are

International Relations

Perceived Benefits

		High	Low
Perceived Costs	**High**	**1** *Hedging* (Singapore)	**2** *Balancing* (Australia)
	Low	**3** *Bandwagoning* (Thailand)	**4** *Buck-passing* (New Zealand)

Figure 1 The "preference-for-change" model of states' policy choices during international order transition

also aware of the potential costs from the order transition. The costs might be generated from the change itself or derived from the future international order.

Therefore, when both the cost and benefit perceptions regarding the order transition are high, policymakers are highly uncertain about the change. It will lead them to adopt a hedging strategy to offset the potential risks associated with the uncertainties. Strategically, this state will choose to befriend both the defenders (the hegemon) and challengers (rising powers) of the existing order at the same time. As mentioned before, it will be a difficult policy choice after the strategic rivalry between the hegemon and the rising powers intensifies because this state will face pressure from both sides.

Cell 2 suggests a situation in which policymakers perceive low benefits but high costs from the international order transition. This cost–benefit calculation will orient policymakers to prefer the status quo to change because any change or transition in the international order will place the state in a worse-off situation. Therefore, policymakers are more likely to choose a "balancing" strategy to countervail any challenges to the existing international order. Since a rising power is normally seen as a revisionist state no matter whether it is right or not (He et al., 2021), this state is more likely to align with the incumbent hegemon to cope with rising powers' challenges. Again, in practice this balancing strategy can be either military, nonmilitary or both.

Cell 3 indicates a situation in which policymakers perceive a low cost but a high benefit from the international order transition. It means that a state will gain more or even be a winner after the international order transition. Therefore, this state will prefer "change" to the status quo during the period of order transition. On policy choices, this state is more likely to pick a "bandwagoning" strategy to embrace and welcome the international order transition. Again, since rising powers are more likely to challenge the existing international order, it means that this state is more likely to cooperate with rising powers to take on the hegemon or ruling powers in the system.

In Cell 4, policymakers perceive both the costs and the benefits from the international order transition at a low level. It means that this state does not care about the international order transition. Or we can say that the potential order transition might not have much impact on the state's national interests. Although the international order transition will influence all states in theory, the perceived impact from the change is different and relative in nature. States have various self-perceived national interests in the world. For example, the South Pacific countries are worried more about climate change than the strategic competition between the United States and China because climate change poses more of an existential threat to the survival of these states than great power competition. It is not to suggest that the South Pacific states do not care about US–China competition. They do care but they might have other priorities in their cost–benefit calculation regarding national interests.

Therefore, a state is more likely to choose a "buck-passing" strategy to avoid the risk associated with the order transition if its policymakers perceive low costs and low benefits from international order transition. In practice, this state will stay away from the strategic competition between rising powers and the incumbent hegemon/ruling powers. Unlike hedging that is a proactive policy to neutralize risks, buck-passing is a passive and wait-and-see policy aiming to avoid risks.

The following are four testable hypotheses of the "preference-for-change" model:

H1. When a state's policymakers are uncertain about the future outcomes of international order transition, this state is more likely to choose a "hedging" strategy so that it can offset the potential risks by working with both challengers and defenders of the international order.

H2. If a state's policymakers perceive net costs (costs > benefits) regarding the international order transition, this state is more likely to choose a "balancing" strategy so that it can work closely with the incumbent powers to countervail threats from rising powers and protect the status quo of the international order.

H3. If a state's policymakers perceive net benefits (costs < benefits) regarding the order transition, this state is more likely to choose a "bandwagoning" strategy so that it can pursue more "profits" by working closely with rising powers to upend the existing international order.

H4. If a state's policymakers perceive both low benefits and low costs regarding the order transition, this state is more likely to choose a "buck-passing" strategy so that it can avoid risks by staying away from the strategic competition between rising powers and ruling powers.

In order to test the validity of this "preference-for-change" model, we conduct four short case studies by examining the policy choices of Singapore, Australia, Thailand, and New Zealand against the background of US–China strategic competition after 2008. All four states have relatively close security ties with the United States. Australia and Thailand are official military allies of the United States. Although the New Zealand-United States alliance was suspended in the mid-1980s due to the nuclear ship dispute (Pugh, 1989; Catalinac, 2010), New Zealand is still in the "Five Eyes" – an intelligence alliance with the United States. Singapore is a quasi-ally of the United States because of their close security cooperation.

We perform a "hard case" or "less-likely-case" testing on our "preference-for-change" model by focusing on these four countries (Eckstein, 1975, pp. 118–19; George & Bennett, 2004). Since all four countries are US allies or security partners, they should choose a similar policy option toward China, which is to balance against China's rise. However, if our case studies show that our model can explain the diverse policy choices of these four US security allies/partners, then we can be confident in arguing that other non-US allies or partners in the region will be more likely to behave according to our model. In other words, if our model can pass or even partially pass these "hard cases," we will be more confident in generalizing our findings to other states in the region. In the concluding section, we employ the preference-for-change model to preliminarily examine other second-tier states' policy choices, which can further test and strengthen the external validity of the model.

To a certain extent, these four case studies also construct a structured, focused comparison for us to rule out some competing variables in explaining states' foreign policy choices during the period of order transition in the international system (George & Bennett, 2004). For example, both Singapore and New Zealand are small powers in terms of economic and military capabilities. Since they have chosen different strategies, as we suggest in the case studies, the size or power of a country will not be a key variable in explaining states' policy choices. Similarly, New Zealand and Australia are both liberal democracies. However, their policy choices between the United States and China also differ significantly in that Australia is more actively siding with the United

States against China's challenge than New Zealand. It means that the democratic system alone cannot fully explain a country's diverging policy choices between the United States and China during the order transition.

In our case studies, we rely on primary data (official documents and leaders' statements) to measure the dynamics of leaders' perceptions of international order transition and employ a process-tracing technique to examine how the changing perceptions of the potential order transition shape a state's policy choices between the United States and China. For each case, the evolution and change of a state's foreign policy choices can be seen as a within-case comparison through which we can confidently control other variables and test the internal validity of our preference-for-change model in explaining a state's policy decisions against the background of US–China strategic competition in the period of order transition in the international system.

It is worth noting that there are some exceptional cases beyond the explanatory power of the preference-for-change model. For example, Taiwan and North Korea face imminent security threats from either China or the United States because of either historical or ideological reasons. The policy choices in these cases will be easily explained by the balance-of-threat logic without examining their leaders' perceptual preferences for the order transition. However, if applying the preference-for-change model to these exceptional states, we can also easily reach the convergent result with the traditional balance of threat theory. In other words, under an extreme security threat situation, our preference-for-change model will reach the same conclusion as balance of threat theory because both theories are rooted in structural realism, especially neorealism, emphasizing the security constraints of the anarchic international system on state behavior.

3 Singapore: Hedging to Cope with Uncertainties

As the smallest state in Southeast Asia, Singapore's policymakers have naturally inherited a strong vulnerability in both strategic and economic senses. In addition, its unique location in the Malacca Strait increases Singapore's strategic sensitivity to great power politics. As Yuen Foong Khong (1999) suggests, Singapore is a "classic anticipatory state" in that policymakers are more likely to make long-term strategic plans according to the changing strategic environment.

During the Cold War, Singapore firmly joined the anti-communist camp, receiving both security protection and economic benefits from the Western world (Leifer, 2000; Ganesan, 2005; Acharya, 2008). After the Cold War, the United States became the only superpower in a newly configured unipolar world. Although some pundits and scholars question how long the United States will enjoy the "unipolar moment" (Krauthammer, 1990), Singaporean policymakers seemed to foresee the durability of the US-led unipolarity in the international system (Leifer, 2000; Ganesan, 2005). Despite the fact that the Philippines shut down its US military base due to burgeoning nationalism, Singapore signed the Memorandum of Understanding Regarding United States Use of Facilities in Singapore in 1990, which supported the continued security presence of the United States in Southeast Asia.

Given that Singapore is a beneficiary of the US-led international order, its foreign policy has simply followed the realist logic of the post–Cold War era (Leifer, 2000; Ganesan, 2005; Acharya, 2008). This logic is to support US hegemony and military presence in the region although it is not an official military ally of the United States. There is a shared perception among Singapore elites that the US leadership or hegemony plays a key role in protecting security and prosperity in the region, especially for Singapore, which is surrounded by two Malay-Muslim countries (Malaysia and Indonesia) in Southeast Asia. As a trading state, the free and open trading system promoted by the United States through the World Trade Organization (WTO) is also vital for Singapore's economy. Therefore, it is a rational decision for Singapore to support US-led international order by keeping strong and close security cooperation with the United States in the post–Cold War era.

During the US war on terror after the September 11, 2001 tragedies, the United States invited Singapore to become a non-NATO ally, but Singapore declined partly because it did not want to cause suspicions from its neighbors and partly because it wished to adhere to its non-aligned principle in foreign policy (Tan, 2011, 2016). However, in 2006, US Secretary of Defense Ashton Carter publicly stated that America has "no better friend than Singapore" in the region (Chow, 2016, cited by Tan, 2016, p. 33). It means that in the eyes of US policymakers, Singapore might – to a certain extent – have even closer security ties with the United States than its treaty allies, like Thailand and the Philippines.

The 2008 Great Financial Crisis (GFC) was widely seen as the beginning of the international order transition because of the US economic turmoil and the rise of the rest (Zakaria, 2008). However, the quick recovery of the US economy in the aftermath of the GFC casted some doubts on how international order transition would unfold. As mentioned before, Singapore is sensitive to the dynamics of international order transition. The Singaporean elites' perceptions of international order transition also experienced some gradual changes. Differing from the popular view that the United States has been in decline since the GFC (Zakaria, 2008; Layne, 2013), Singaporean leaders have been extremely confident that the United States would sustain its hegemony for at least two more decades. Singaporean leaders publicly refuted the coming age of a multipolar world, which seems to be a codeword regarding the end of the unipolarity led by the United States.

For example, Lee Kuan Yew, the founding father of Singapore, publicly stated that:

> multi-polarity where different poles are approximately equal in strategic weight is unlikely to emerge because the "poles" are not equal . . . After the crisis, the US is most likely to remain at the top of every key index of national power for decades. It will remain the dominant global player for the next few decades. (Lee Kuan Yew, 2009)

Lee Kuan Yew's firm denial of multipolarity demonstrated his faith in the unrivaled American primacy even after the GFC. In a similar vein, Singapore's current Prime Minister Lee also firmly stated during the COVID-19 pandemic that:

> the United States is not a declining power. It has great resilience and strengths, one of which is its ability to attract talent from around the world; of the nine people of Chinese ethnicity who have been awarded Nobel Prizes in the sciences, eight were U.S. citizens or subsequently became U.S. citizens. (Lee Hsien Loong, 2020, p. 56)

Believing in US hegemony does not mean that Singaporean leaders deny the potential order transition, especially the rise of China in the international system. Interestingly, Singaporean leaders came to an optimistic view of China's rise and its implications for the existing international order. On the one hand, they perceived a "positive and constructive" relationship between the United States and China during the Obama administration. On the other hand, they believed that China's rise will be gradual and peaceful (Lee Hsien Loong, 2009). More importantly, China will be constrained by the existing international order. For example, Prime Minister Lee Hsien Loong stated in 2010 that "China is still far from being a developed country. It needs US technology, US corporate expertise and, more importantly, a non-adversarial United States which will ensure a stable global environment within which China can continue to develop" (Lee, 2010).

It is worth noting that Singaporean leaders' positive view on China is also strongly backed by the general public in Singapore. In a recent Pew survey conducted in seventeen advanced economies, Singapore is the only country where more people hold a favorable view on China (64 percent) than on the United States (51 percent). Considering China's plummeting image in all other countries in the survey, especially after the COVID-19 pandemic, the strong favorable perception of Singapore on China is even extraordinary (Silver, 2021). It might explain why Singaporean leaders publicly express a positive view on China's rise but at the same time strongly support US military presence in the region as well as US hegemony in the existing international order.

In 2011, the Obama administration launched a "pivot" or "rebalance" toward Asia. In the eyes of Chinese leaders, it was a containment strategy of the United States against China's rise (Lieberthal & Wang, 2012; Yan, 2013). However, Singaporean leaders enthusiastically supported the "US rebalance strategy" while at the same time holding a positive view of US–China relations. In his keynote speech at the 2015 Shangri-La Dialogue, Prime Minister Lee contended that:

> [the US] presence is welcomed by the many regional countries which have benefited from it, including Singapore … President Obama has reaffirmed that America is and always will be a Pacific Power and the Obama Administration has articulated a strategic 'rebalance' towards Asia … China's rise has been peaceful, within the established international order. The key to this peaceful rise continuing is the US-China relationship (Lee Hsien Loong, 2015).

In other words, Singaporean policymakers do not deny the reality of order transition driven by China's rise. However, they believe that China's rise is just part of an internal adjustment of the existing international order, which will still be led by the United States.

As a result of the optimistic view of international order transition with strong confidence in US hegemony and simultaneously a favorable view on China's rise, Singapore holds an ambiguous cost-and-benefit perception regarding the international order transition. In our model, Singapore is placed in Cell 1 because its policymakers expect both high costs (the decline of US power) and high benefits (the rise of China) from the potential order transition. Therefore, according to our model, Singapore is more likely to choose a hedging strategy with a combination of military balancing and economic bandwagoning in order to cope with the uncertainties of the order transition (Kuik, 2008). In reality, we see a typical hedging strategy of Singapore by walking "the strategic tightrope between the US and China nimbly" (Lam, 2020, p. 157).

In the security domain, Singapore enthusiastically supported the US rebalance strategy and strengthened its military ties with the United States. In 2005, Singapore and the United States upgraded their security partnership through the establishment of the "US-Singapore Strategic Framework Agreement," which covered joint exercises, cooperation on US peacekeeping operations, and access to US defense technology. In 2012, Singapore agreed to allow the US Navy to deploy four new warships – the littoral combat ships – to Singapore. In 2016, Singapore permitted the United States to deploy two P-8A Poseidon maritime patrol aircraft from the US Seventh Fleet for surveillance missions (Tan, 2016). Although the Obama administration publicly denied that the US rebalance strategy targeted China, it is an open secret that China viewed it as a containment strategy against its rise. Therefore,

Singapore's strengthened military ties with the United States can be seen as military balancing efforts against China.

In the political arena, Singapore and the United States jointly established the US-Singapore Strategic Partnership Dialogue (SPD) in 2012 in order to "move up a weight class" for the bilateral relations (Tan, 2016, p. 27). The SPD later became a major platform for Singapore to coordinate its foreign policy with the United States, for instance on the TPP and the South China Sea issue. For example, Singapore strongly supported the United States to lead the TPP negotiation, which is seen as an economic counterbalance against China's increasing economic clout in the region. Moreover, Singapore publicly joined the United States and Western countries to support the South China Sea arbitration brought by the Philippines against China. Although it is consistent with Singapore's long-time emphasis on international laws, this behavior is still seen as a direct challenge or political balancing against China's behavior in the South China Sea. It is also the key reason for the diplomatic flare-ups between China and Singapore in the mid-2010s (Chong, 2017; Emmerson, 2018).

However, economically Singapore has kept a close relationship with China. Singapore supported China's AIIB initiative in 2012 and endorsed China's BRI in 2013 although it does not need infrastructural funds like other Southeast Asian countries (Ba, 2019; Chan, 2019). As Irene Chan points out, Singapore's participation in the BRI is a case of "reverse BRI flow," which means that Singapore does not receive loans and investment from China. Instead, it invests in the development of China's western region, especially Chongqing. Why is Singapore so supportive of China's BRI, which is widely criticized by the United States and other Western countries? The answer lies in Singaporean leaders' positive views on China's rise as well as the future of BRI. As Trade Minister Chan Chun Sing stated at the 2018 World Economic Forum in Davos, with the BRI, China is "helping the world to build a better system that allows the world to participate in the next phase of growth in the economy" (World Economic Forum, 2018, cited by Chan, 2019, p. 190). Therefore, Singapore's "economic bandwagoning" with the BRI as well as China in general is rooted in Singaporean leaders' positive perceptions of China's rise, especially the benefits that China's rise can bring to Singapore and the region.

A hedging strategy is a rational and relatively easy choice for small and middle powers to make if the United States and China can keep their strategic competition and rivalry on an even keel. After Trump came to power in 2017, the US–China relations experienced a dramatic downturn in all dimensions. Along with increasing tensions and even antagonism between the two nations in the period of order transition, the room for Singapore to freely maneuver between the United States and China has shrunk even further. As one Singaporean commentator points out, "there is no sweet spot to keep both Beijing and Washington happy, but that has not kept Singapore from trying" (Choong, 2021). Singapore will stick to this hedging strategy as long as it holds an ambiguous cost-and-benefit perception regarding the international order transition. It is also why Singapore not only supported Biden's IPEF initiative but also publicly endorsed China's application to join the Comprehensive and Progressive Agreement for Trans-Pacific Partnership (CPTPP) and the Digital Economy Partnership Agreement. However, Singapore might have to make a choice between the United States and China and move beyond the current "hedging" strategy after its political leaders eventually make up their minds about their preference for change regarding the order transition in the future.

4 Australia: Balancing to Resist Change

As a traditional ally of the United States, Australia is a strong supporter of the rules-based international order led by the United States. Kevin Rudd, then-Australian Prime Minister, claimed that "promoting global rules-based order" is one of Australia's five "national security interests" in his 2008 National Security Speech (Rudd, 2008). In the 2009 *Defence White Paper* (DWP), the term appeared ten times. "A stable, rules-based global security order" is defined as one of Australia's four "strategic interests" (DoD, 2009). In the 2013 DWP, the phrase "rules-based order" was mentioned eleven times, while remaining in the strategic interest list of Australia (DoD, 2013). Three years later, the "rules-based order" became a buzz phrase in Australia's policy discourse. It appeared fifty-six times in the 2016 DWP, in which "a stable Indo-Pacific region and a rules-based global order" was defined as one of Australia's three "strategic defence interests." It means that Australia would have been willing to use force to protect them if needed (DoD, 2016; Bisley & Schreer, 2018, p. 306).[9] The 2016 DWP also provides a clear definition of the "rules-based" order for Australia. It specifies that:

> A rules-based global order means a shared commitment by all countries to conduct their activities in accordance with agreed rules which evolve over time, such as international law and regional security arrangements. This shared commitment has become even more important with growing

---

[9] The other two strategic interests in the 2016 DWP are "a secure, resilient Australia, with secure northern approaches and proximate sea lines of communication" and "a secure nearer region, encompassing maritime South East Asia and South Pacific (comprising Papua New Guinea, Timor-Leste and Pacific Island Countries)": DoD (2016, p. 33).

interconnectivity, which means that events across the world have the potential to affect Australia's security and prosperity. (DoD, 2016, p. 15)

There are two reasons for the Australian government to highlight the "rules-based order" in the official document. First, it reflects the strategic anxiety of Australian policymakers over the existing international order. The mere reason for them to emphasize the order is that they are fully aware of its ongoing and inevitable transition. As Nick Bisley points out, in the eyes of Australian policymakers, US preponderant military power is seen as the key guarantee of the rules-based order (Bisley, 2017). For Australian policymakers US primacy is *the* balance of power in the world. Any challenge to US primacy is a threat to the "balance" of the international order as a whole. For example, in the *2017 Foreign Policy White Paper*, it is stated on page 1 that "[T]he United States has been the dominant power in our region throughout Australia's post-Second World War history. Today, China is challenging America's position" (DFAT, 2017, p. 1). It is clear that Australian policymakers have attached a negative connotation to even the very notion of order transition caused by China because of the indicative potentiality of future instability and conflict in the international system.

Second, by emphasizing the rules-based order, Australian policymakers have also revealed their latent but strong strategic preference for defending the status quo of the international order. Australian policymakers have mixed feelings about China's booming economic power, given that its policy behavior is seen as a negative force against the rules and norms of the existing international order. The rules-based order in the minds of Australian policymakers specifically refers to the rules and norms embedded in the UN-centered institutions and the Bretton Woods system, such as the UNCLOS, the human rights declaration as well as the open market and free trading regime. To a certain extent, all these institutions were built on and maintained by US primacy after the Second World War.[10] As Nick Bisley points out, "[I]n many ways the 'rules-based international order' – understood as a shorthand for the UN-centered system that imposes limits on what states can do and which provides a wide array of rules governing international economic relations – is the only international environment Australia has known" (Bisley, 2018).

---

[10] It should be noted that even though Australia emphasizes the rules-based international order, it does not clearly define what these rules are and whose order to follow. On the contrary, at the Alaska meeting in March 2021 China made it clear that the Chinese understanding of the international order is the UN-based rules, not the US ones. Australia's ambiguity on the rules-based order reveals its strategic dilemma in the international order. It is that as a middle power, Australia should cherish UN-based multilateralism, but as a military ally, it has to follow the US lead.

As the only industrialized economy with uninterrupted economic growth during the 2008 GFC, Australia has felt very blessed by the existing rules and institutions. It is a public consensus that Australia's economic prosperity has heavily depended on multilateral institutions, especially bilateral and multilateral trade arrangements. Besides the UN-related institutions, Australia has also actively participated in the G20, the TPP (the later CPTPP), and the Regional Comprehensive Economic Partnership (RCEP). All these "rules-based" institutional benefits Australia has enjoyed are seen to stem from US leadership. It further reinforces the importance of US primacy in Australia's views on the rules-based international order.

During the period 2016–2020, one notable development of Australia's views on the rules-based order is the emergence of normative values in the official discourse. The expression of "normative values" refers particularly to democracy and liberalism. While the 2013 DWP only mentioned the "values" once in reference to NATO, the word "values" appeared seven times in the 2016 DWP (DoD, 2013, 2016). It is worth noting that the 2016 DWP did not link values with liberalism or democracy explicitly. As Bisley and Schreer point out, Australia's deliberate separation between "liberal" and "rules-based order" is to "implicitly contain an offer of cooperation to non-democratic Asia-Pacific countries" (Bisley & Schreer, 2018, p. 312), because emphasizing liberalism and democracy might alienate some Asian states, which are either not full democracies or not embracing liberal norms and culture, especially Singapore and Vietnam.

However, this cautious and prudent attitude changed dramatically in 2017. In the 2017 FPWP, "values had gone mainstream" (Reilly, 2020). The term "values" was mentioned thirty-one times, including a subsection entitled "Australia's values." More specifically, it suggests that "Australia does not define its national identity by race or religion, but by shared values, including political, economic and religious freedom, liberal democracy, the rule of law, racial and gender equality and mutual respect" (DFAT, 2017, p. 11). In addition, "Australia's values are a critical component of the foundation upon which we build our international engagement. Our support for political, economic and religious freedoms, liberal democracy, the rule of law, racial and gender equality and mutual respect reflect who we are and how we approach the world" (DFAT, 2017, pp. 2–3).

However, Australian politicians also realize the inevitable transition or transformation of the current international order given the rise and fall of great powers in the international system. In 2016, Turnbull warned in his speech at the Lowy Institute that Australia was experiencing "[a] pace of transformation unknown, unprecedented in scale and pace in all of human history" (Turnbull, 2016). During the 2020 COVID-19 pandemic, Morrison stated that "we have not seen the conflation of global, economic and strategic uncertainty now being experienced here in Australia in our region since the existential threat we faced when the global and regional order collapsed in the 1930s and 1940s" (Morrison, 2020). Moreover, Morrison believes that Australia is in the epicenter of the rising strategic competition in the Indo-Pacific, which is "under increasing – and … almost irreversible – strain" (Morrison, 2020).

China, as a rising power, is seen as the main challenger to the rules-based order that Australia has cherished for decades. Australia is concerned over the ongoing transition in three ways. First, China's rise has altered the power configuration in the international system, shifting away from unipolarity, and this change brings about uncertainties. Consequently, China is perceived by Australian policy-makers as an inevitable challenge to the leadership of the United States, which is considered a key stabilizer of the international order. As the 2017 FPWP states, "powerful drivers of change are converging in a way that is re-shaping the international order and challenging Australian interests" (DFAT, 2017, p. 1). In particular, "navigating the decade ahead will be hard because, as China's power grows, our region is changing in ways without precedent in Australia's modern history" (DFAT, 2017, p. 4). In other words, the rise of China is perceived to bring about unprecedented transformations within the international system, accompanied by a multitude of uncertainties and anxieties for Australia.

Second, China's assertive behavior in the South China Sea and the East China Sea after 2010 has been regarded as serious revisionist behavior against the UNCLOS in particular and current international order in general by Australian policymakers. For example, the 2016 DWP clearly stated that "Australia is particularly concerned by the unprecedented pace and scale of China's land reclamation activities" (DoD, 2016, p. 58). In addition, it condemned China's 2013 unilateral declaration of an Air Defence Identification Zone in the East China Sea, because it "caused tensions to rise. Australia is opposed to any coercive or unilateral actions to change the status quo in the East China Sea" (DoD, 2016, p. 61). Moreover, Australia has pushed China to abide by the ruling of the arbitral tribunal on the South China Sea dispute between the Philippines and China in 2016 (DFAT, 2017, p. 47).

In the 2020 Strategic Update document, China was again portraited as a typical revisionist against the current rules-based order. It stated that:

> since 2016, major powers have become more assertive in advancing their strategic preferences and seeking to exert influence, including China's active pursuit of greater influence in the Indo-Pacific. Australia is concerned by the potential for actions, such as the establishment of military bases, which could undermine stability in the Indo-Pacific and our immediate region. (DoD, 2020, p. 11)

Here China is the only country mentioned as being "more assertive" in the Indo-Pacific after 2016. It is apparent that China is not only seen as a direct challenge to US primacy but also treated as a revisionist power against the whole "rules-based" order underpinned by US leadership.

Last but not least, China is seen as standing on the opposite side of the liberal values. As mentioned above, Australia's foreign policy has taken a "value" turn since 2017. As a liberal democracy, it is understandable for Australia to be proud of its "values," especially liberalism and democracy. However, Australia's high-profile return to values in foreign policy is more strategic than just rhetorical. As Reilly suggests, Australia's embrace of the word "values" mainly aims to target China and especially the CCP, because China is seen as having become more authoritarian in domestic politics and more assertive in international affairs under Xi Jinping's leadership (Reilly, 2020). China's negative reaction to the ruling of the Permanent Court of Arbitration (PCA) in the Hague has also convinced Australian leaders that China is a revisionist power challenging the liberal values. More importantly, this value-based foreign policy has become a bipartisan consensus between the Coalition and the Labor Party in Australia (Reilly, 2020). Consequently, China's rise or China-led potential order transition has become a severe challenge or threat to Australia's value-oriented foreign policy.

It is worth noting that Australia used to maintain a hedging strategy between the United States and China, just like Singapore (Chan 2020; Wilkins 2023). On the one hand, Australia has strengthened its security ties with the United States. On the other hand, it has benefited significantly from China's economic rise. In late 2007, China overtook Japan to become Australia's largest trading partner. In 2009, China became Australia's largest export market, while Australia was China's seventh-largest trading partner. In 2014, the two countries signed the China-Australia free trade agreement, which entered into force in December 2015. In the same year, the leaders of Australia and China officially described their bilateral relations as a "comprehensive strategic partnership," signifying high-level close ties between the two countries in economic, political, and even security areas.

However, Australia–China relations began to sour gradually in the second part of the 2010s. In December 2017, then Australian Prime Minister Malcolm Turnbull stated that the Australian people would "stand up" against China after introducing new espionage and foreign interference legislation. In 2020, the Morrison government publicly called for an independent investigation into the origins of COVID-19 a few months after the pandemic became common knowledge. It was seen as both a diplomatic and a political provocation by

Chinese leaders. Consequently, China slapped tariffs and unofficial bans on a range of Australian exports, such as barley, beef, and wine, and also imposed a freeze on high-level talks. Since then, bilateral relations between the two nations have deteriorated dramatically.

How to explain the dramatic downturn of the Australia–China relations? Our preference-for-change model can shed some light from the Australian side. As we discussed before, the Australian government has gradually deepened its negative view of the potential order transition caused by China's rise since the 2008 GFC. In the cost–benefit calculation, the order transition apparently embodies high costs and low benefits for Australian policymakers. It places Australian policymakers in Cell 2 in the "preference-for-change" model in Figure 1 as an example of resistance against change. According to our model, Australia is more likely to conduct a "balancing" strategy to work with the incumbent hegemon and ruling powers to defend the existing international order. In reality, Australia has conducted a series of balancing strategies against China's challenge to the international order in recent years.

First, by increasing its military budget Australia has conducted an "internal balancing" strategy against China's challenge to the international order (Waltz, 1979). Since 2016 Australia has increased its military budget (DoD, 2016). More importantly, it has ensured a long-term commitment to defense spending. As some scholars point out, the 2016 DWP actually broke the 2 percent of GDP as the defense spending target because the 2016 DWP clearly states that "the 10-year funding model … will not be subject to any further adjustments as a result of changes in Australia's GDP growth esti- mates" (Baldino & Carr, 2016). During the pandemic, the Morrison govern- ment released a defense budget update in July 2020, in which Australia pledged to increase its defense budget significantly. More specifically, it stated that Australia will increase its defense budget to A\$73.7 billion over the next ten years in 2029–2030, with total funding of A\$575 billion over the decade (DoD, 2020, p. 7). Why did Australia decide to increase its military budget when the economy was hard hit by the pandemic? Morrison explained that it was to prepare "for a post-COVID world that is poorer, that is more dangerous, and that is more disorderly" (Morrison, 2020). Although he did not explicitly mention any country's name in his speech, China is definitely the "usual suspect" behind Australia's drastic military build-up during the pandemic.

This internal balancing strategy also closely links to Australia's "external balancing" through strengthening its military alliance and security cooperation with like-minded countries in the Indo-Pacific. Besides augmenting its "100- year mateship" with the United States, Australia actively advocated a minilateral security arrangement through reviving the Quadrilateral Security

Dialogue – the so-called Quad 2.0 – in 2017 (Tow, 2019). The Quad 1.0 as an informal security dialogue mechanism was established by four countries, including Australia, Japan, India, and the United States, in 2007. However, Australia under the Rudd administration unilaterally withdrew from the Quad 1.0 in 2008 out of concern over China's objection.

In 2017, senior security officials from the Quad countries reinvigorated the Quad 2.0 by meeting on the sidelines of the East Asia Summit. Australia has played a proactive role in advocating security cooperation through the Quad 2.0 framework. In September 2019, the Quad 2.0 was elevated from a senior official gathering to a ministerial-level meeting in that the foreign ministers from the four nations met on the sidelines of the UN General Assembly. One week later, Morrison highly praised the upgrade of the Quad 2.0 in his Lowy lecture by stating, "it is a key forum for exchanging views on challenges facing the region, including taking forward practical cooperation on maritime, terrorism and cyber issues" (Morrison, 2019). Since the Quad 2.0 is a typical minilateral arrangement, focusing on regional security issues, it well complements the US traditional bilateralism-based hub-and-spokes system in the regional security architecture (Tow, 2019). In March 2021, the Quad 2.0 was further elevated to an annual leaders' summit, despite virtually for the first time during COVID-19. In September 2021, the establishment of AUKUS, a new security pact among Australia, the United Kingdom and the United States, has been described as a "Rubicon moment" for Australia's foreign policy (Westcott, 2021).

Last, Australia has launched its "ideological balancing" policy to target the CCP's "sharp power" – political influence – in Australia. Australia is the first country to pass a foreign interference law to implicitly block the CCP's political influence. Australia is the first country to ban Huawei from participating in its own 5G telecommunications system due to national security concerns (Bagshaw & Harris, 2019; Gyngell, 2019). In her 2017 Fullerton lecture in Singapore, then-foreign minister Julie Bishop targeted China's political system by highlighting the incompatibility between China's authoritarian rule and liberal democracy (Bishop, 2017). In April 2020, Foreign Minister Marise Payne publicly questioned China's transparency on the COVID-19 outbreak and announced that Australia would push for an investigation into the origins and spread of coronavirus. China criticized Payne's comments as "not based on facts" and treated Australia's call for an open investigation as a "political attack" against the legitimacy of the CCP (Davidson, 2020).

In September 2020, during her speech to the UN's Human Rights Council, Foreign Minister Payne harshly criticized the Chinese government for enforcing "repressive measures" against Uyghurs in Xinjiang and for eroding rights and freedoms in Hong Kong. In the eyes of Chinese diplomats, Australia's accusations reflect its "typical double standards" on human rights as well as a "blatant smear against China" (Hurst, 2020). The bilateral relationship between Australia and China continued to deteriorate until the Australian Labor Party won the general election and came to power in late May 2022. Although the Albanese-Xi meeting at the G20 in November officially ended the "diplomatic freeze" between the two countries, the future of the Australia–China relationship is still full of uncertainties. Australian political elites, no matter whether from liberal or conservative party ideology, will not change their perceptions of the potential order transition and China's rise overnight.

In sum, Australian policymakers cherish the existing rules-based international order and hold a negative perception regarding the potential order transition. This high-cost and low-benefit calculation of the order transition drives them to choose a "balancing" strategy to fight against China – the order challenger, especially when US–China strategic rivalry intensified during the Trump administration. Australia has employed three types of balancing strategies: internal balancing by building up its military capabilities, external balancing by strengthening military and security ties with the United States and other regional security partners via the Quad mechanism, as well as ideological balancing by targeting the CCP political system and authoritarian values. Recent developments in the realm of security provide additional validation for Australia's choice of a "balancing" strategy against China. In early 2022, Australia and Japan signed a security agreement to bolster their defense ties against the backdrop of China's rising military and economic might. In April 2023, Australia announced its defense shape-up plan, which emphasized enhancing its security alliance with the United States by prioritizing long-range strike capabilities, potentially countervailing China's military threats. Australia has apparently chosen to side with the United States against China's rise during the period of international order transition.

5 Thailand: Bandwagoning to Seek Profit

Thailand's foreign policy has been famously characterized as "bamboo diplomacy," which means that it is like "bamboo bending with the wind" with maximum flexibility and pragmatism (Kislenko, 2002; Busbarat, 2016, 2017, 2019). As the only treaty ally of the United States in the mainland of Southeast Asia, Thailand stood firmly in the anti-communist camp with the United States during the Cold War. However, it also worked with China as a *de facto* ally against Vietnam during the Vietnam-Cambodia War in the late 1970s. After the Cold War, like other Southeast Asian countries, Thailand adopted a classic "hedging strategy" to keep its security ties with the United States but to do business with China (Kuik, 2016; Han, 2018; Cogan, 2019).

The potential international order transition in the early twenty-first century, especially after the 2008 GFC, has posed a litmus test for Thailand's "bamboo diplomacy." Will Thailand keep its hedging strategy during the order transition or will it "bend with the wind" to change its policy orientation? If we treat the "international order transition" as the "wind," how the bamboo (Thailand) will bend depends on its political elite's perceptions of the nature of the "wind." Like other countries in this research, Thailand is in full recognition of the upcoming international order transition. However, Thai political elites seem to hold a different and even more visionary view on where the "wind" will go. While the Singaporean and Australian leaders strongly believed in the durability of US hegemony and leadership even after the 2008 GFC, Thai elites have predicted the decline of US power since the late 1990s.

In 1999, Thailand and China signed a "Plan of Action for the Twenty-First Century," aiming to strategically strengthen bilateral relations in almost all issue areas. This official document states that both countries recognized the importance of a "new multipolar security order." As Ann Marie Murphy points out, it is unusual for Thailand – a formal US ally – to use the word "multipolar" in the official document because it implies "a desire for a decline in American power" (Murphy, 2010, p. 12). To a certain extent, it reflects "the disillusionment" of the Thai elite with the US power status in the future international order. In a similar vein, after the 2008 GFC, Thailand's Prime Minister Abhisit Vejjajiva (2009) publicly stated that the "New Global Landscape" is forming and "the Chinese and Indian economies have performed well compared to the rest of the world even in this time of crisis" (Vejjajiva, 2009). Although he did not directly point out the decline of US power, the underlying message is more than clear.

Besides the perception of declining US hegemony, Thai elites have also deepened their negative views on the United States since the 1997–1998 Asian Financial Crisis (AFC). As a treaty ally, the United States failed to provide much-needed support to Thailand as it did toward South Korea (Busbarat, 2016). Instead, the indifferent attitude and heavy-handed pressure of the United States through the IMF caused Thailand's economy to suffer bitterly during the AFC. In addition, the United States declined to support the Thai candidate to compete for the WTO Secretary General position in 1999. As Pongphisoot Busbarat points out, the AFC and its aftermath "crystallized a changing perception of many Thais toward the American commitment to the kingdom … instead of helping, many Thais viewed the United States as have a neo-imperialist agenda … to destabilize the [Thai] economy" (Busbarat, 2017, p. 263).

If Thai elites felt disappointed about the indifferent response from the United States during the AFC, they were irritated by the United States interferences into Thailand's internal affairs. It is worth noting that Thai domestic politics entered an extremely unstable and volatile period characterized by political violence, street protests, and military intervention in the early 2000s. Two military coups took place in 2006 and 2014 respectively. The democratically elected leaders (Thaksin Shinawatra and Yingluck Shinawatra) were ousted from power by the military during the coups. Despite the changes in government from democratically elected leaders to military junta, Thai elites from both civilian and military forces seem to share some negative perceptions on the United States for different reasons.

During the Thaksin era, the United States criticized Thailand's human rights violations, especially Thaksin's iron-handed approach to the southern unrest and the war on drugs. This led Thaksin to publicly describe the United States as an "annoying friend" (Busbarat, 2017, p. 264). After the 2006 coup, the United States not only imposed sanctions on the Thai government but also allegedly became involved in Thai's domestic affairs, including supporting the opposition party and criticizing the Thai government's sentence of an American citizen for insulting the monarchy (Fuller, 2011). Therefore, as Busbarat points out, "negative attitudes toward the United States rose among Thai establishment elites and their royalist mass supporters" in the early 2010s (Busbarat, 2017, p. 266).

The 2014 military coup once again dragged Thailand–US relations to the nadir. The democratically elected Prime Minister Yingluck was removed, and the military declared martial laws to hold onto power. Unlike other coups in the past in which the military normally transferred power to civilian rule within a year, the military junta delayed the general election until March 2019. Consequently, the Obama administration imposed the harshest sanctions on Thailand, including publicly denouncing the junta, suspending military assistance, and downsizing military exercises and cooperation (Storey, 2015, 2019; Busbarat, 2016, 2017). After Trump came to power in 2017, the United States gradually restored its military cooperation with Thailand because Trump unlike Obama did not care much about Thailand's anti-democracy and human rights record. However, as Ian Storey points out, US–Thailand relations became the "main victim" of the 2014 coup (Storey, 2015, p. 6). One survey of 1800 mainly military Thai officials conducted in 2015–2017 suggests that the United States was seen as "the greatest military threat" to Thailand (Blaxland & Raymond, 2017). It is clear that United States interference in Thai domestic politics, especially after the 2014 coup, is the major reason for this strong negative view of the United States among Thai military officials.

China, however, is perceived more positively among Thai elites. First, China's responsible and generous support to Thailand during the 1997–1998 AFC is in sharp contrast with the United States. Unlike the United States seen as only a "fair weather friend," China is treated as a friend-in-need who can provide support during economic crises (Sussangkarn, 2011; Storey, 2015, p. 2). Second, China stayed away from Thailand's domestic politics, especially regarding the military coups in 2006 and 2014. In the eyes of Thai elites, including both democratic leaders and military juntas, China and other Asian countries are more understanding about the importance of stability for Thailand than the United States. Instead of imposing sanctions on Thailand after the coups, China provided military and economic support during the crises (Murphy, 2010; Hewison, 2018; Storey, 2019).

For example, after the 2006 coup, China offered US$49 million to Thailand after the United States cut military aid worth US$24 million (Murphy, 2010, p. 13). In December 2014, Chinese Premier Li Keqiang visited Thailand, becoming the highest ranking foreign leader to visit Thailand after the coup. Li's visit significantly strengthened the political legitimacy of the military junta when it faced harsh condemnations from the West, led by the United States. Moreover, China signed two MOUs with the Thailand government during Li's visit, which also provided much-needed economic support to Thailand. As some scholars point out, it is a widespread misunderstanding that the 2014 military coup is a "critical juncture" of the rapid development of China–Thailand relations. In reality, Thailand has been tilting toward China for a long time before the 2014 coup (Hewison, 2018). The 2014 coup, however, triggered the bilateral relations between China and Thailand to move "from strength to strength," especially on military cooperation (Storey, 2019).

Therefore, comparing the different perceptions of the United States and China, we can safely argue that Thai elites prefer "change" or "international order transition" to the "status quo" led by US hegemony in the international system. The rise of China is not seen as a security threat or a source of instability to Thailand because the two countries do not have territorial or maritime disputes. In addition, China's charm offensive in the post–Cold War era indeed paid off in Thailand in that both democratic leaders and military elites generally view China as a "valued and reliable political, economic, and military partner" (Storey, 2015, p. 2). Therefore, the potential international order transition in which China might replace US leadership in the international system is not only acceptable but even welcomed by Thai leaders, especially when the United States has been pressuring Thailand on multiple fronts.

In our "preference-for-change" model, Thailand is placed in Cell 3 in Figure 1 in which political leaders perceive high benefits and low costs regarding the international order transition. Therefore, our model suggests that Thailand is more likely to choose a "bandwagoning" strategy to accommodate the rising power of China. In reality, Thailand has indeed strengthened its economic and military ties with China in the post–Cold War era, especially since the 2000s. More importantly, Thailand's bandwagoning strategy is not just for economic interests like other countries in Southeast Asia, but at the expense of its security alliance with the United States.

First, Thailand was lukewarm toward the Obama administration's pivot or rebalance toward Asia policy in 2011. As some scholars point out, Thailand is "the only US ally still 'mute' to the US pivot" (Chongkittavorn, 2015). "Neither democratic leader nor military successor has evinced genuine enthusiasm for America's pivot" because of the divergent threat perceptions between Thailand and the United States regarding China's rise (Storey, 2015, p. 10). After the 2014 coup, while the United States cut military aid and stopped arms sales to Thailand, China agreed to supply three diesel-electric submarines for US\$1.03 billion and forty-eight marine battle tanks.

Moreover, Thailand and China conducted joint military exercises and strengthened military training and exchange programs. It is reported that from 2005 to 2019, Thailand and China conducted thirteen bilateral and fourteen multilateral military exercises. Ironically, as a US treaty ally, Thailand has participated in more combined military exercises with China than any other Southeast Asian country (Storey, 2019, p. 6). Besides the quantity, the two countries also improved the quality of military exercises. For example, the "Blue Strike" military exercise in 2016 was seen as the most comprehensive war game the two have ever had, including land and sea operations, amphibious training, disaster relief, and counter-terrorism drills (Han, 2018; Hewison, 2018).

It is worth noting that in comparison with the US–Thailand military alliance, the China–Thailand security cooperation might look pale in a general sense (Hewison, 2018; Storey, 2019). However, as a US treaty ally, Thailand's military ties with China will inevitably impose substantial costs to the US alliance system in the region. For example, in 2012 Thailand under the Yingluck administration tactfully rejected a proposal from US space agency NASA to use its U-Tapao airbase for climate change research. It is reported that Yingluck's reluctance stemmed from an unspoken concern that "NASA's request was a ruse by Washington to increase its military presence in Southeast Asia to contain China" (Busbarat, 2016, p. 247).

In May 2015, Thailand under the junta government refused a US request to use its airbase to conduct surveillance missions to monitor Rohingya refugees. Although later it did allow US aircraft to use Thai airspace, the US mission was escorted by a Thai aircraft (Storey, 2015, p. 12). As mentioned above, Thailand is the only treaty ally of the United States in the mainland Southeast Asia. However, given Thailand's close military ties with China, the United States can no longer take access to Thailand's military bases for granted. As a former US defense attaché to Thailand pointed out, Thai restrictions on the "unfettered access that was historically granted to the US forces" were detrimental to Obama's pivot strategy (Walton, 2015, cited by Storey, 2015, pp. 12–13).

Besides military cooperation, Thailand has also bandwagoned with China through accommodating its political and economic interests. For example, in July 2015 the junta deported 109 Uyghurs, partially at the request of China. This policy move can be seen as Thailand's political bandwagoning with China. The United States and the UN immediately condemned Thailand's decision as "a flagrant violation of international law" (Cogan, 2019, p. 34). Economically, Thailand not only takes advantage of China's rise for its own trade and economic growth but also supports China's economic and strategic initiatives enthusiastically, such as the BRI and AIIB. When Premier Li visited Thailand in 2014, one MOU signed between the two countries was a railway project through the "strategic framework for development of Thailand's transportation infrastructure 2015–2022." This proposed Thai-Chinese railway project was claimed as the key part of China's BRI strategy to link Kunming to Singapore although it has faced numerous domestic and economic difficulties (Hewison, 2018).

Thailand is also a strong supporter of the RCEP – a regional free trade agreement endorsed by China, which is seen as a competing economic institution against the US-led TPP. Because it intentionally excluded China, the TPP was widely treated as an economic arm of Obama's pivot strategy against China. Again, Thailand became an outlier among US treaty allies because it showed little interest in the TPP. It was reported that Thailand was reluctant to join the TPP negotiation despite having been approached by the United States numerous times (Busbarat, 2016). After the 2014 coup, the TPP door was technically shut for Thailand because it was listed as a Tier 3 country in the US Trafficking in Person Report in 2015. By law, the US government cannot negotiate trade deals, including the TPP, with Tier 3 countries (Storey, 2015). However, the US loss of Thailand in the TPP became a Chinese gain in the RCEP. To a certain extent, Thailand's economic bandwagoning with China in the RCEP has technically reduced the economic impact of Obama's pivot or rebalance strategy in Asia.

Despite being a military ally of the United States, Thailand did not choose a balancing strategy against China like Australia because of Thai leaders' different perceptions of China's rise. Rather than treating China as a security threat, Thai elites view China as an economic opportunity and even a security partner. As our "preference-for-change" model suggests, Thailand basically chose a "bandwagoning" strategy to accommodate the rise of China and pursue economic and military profits brought by the potential order transition in the post-GFC era. Thailand's bandwagoning with China has gradually derailed its alliance relationship with the United States. In other words, Thailand's band-wagoning with China is not just a cautious measure to offset the potential risks without any harm to US interests – it is actually at the expense of US strategic interests in the region.

In Thailand's recent national election held on May 14, 2023, the opposition parties, namely Move Forward and Pheu Thai, emerged victorious by a substantial margin over their conservative and military-backed counterparts. It is noteworthy that the Election Commission holds the responsibility of formally certifying the results within a timeframe of sixty days, after which the selection of a prime minister will take place. Irrespective of the future developments in the coming months, the military will wield significant influence in shaping the forthcoming Thai government. Within the realm of foreign policy, Thailand will face new challenges in re-navigating its choice between the United States and China amidst the backdrop of the intensified strategic competition between the two in the Indo-Pacific region.

6 New Zealand: Buck-Passing to Avoid Risks

New Zealand shares many characteristics with Singapore in terms of population, dependence on international trade, as well as international status. One key difference, however, is the vulnerability of national security. Unlike Singapore surrounded by two Muslim-majority countries and located in a strategic chokepoint in Southeast Asia, New Zealand is isolated in the South Pacific. This geographical isolation is a natural advantage to separate New Zealand from military conflicts in other regions.

Therefore, as the former Prime Minister Bill English (2016–2017) famously stated, New Zealand holds a sense of "naïve kiwi optimism" regarding the international order transition in the context of US–China strategic rivalry because "we can't control any of that environment" (English, 2017). In other words, even though recognizing the potential turbulent order transition, New Zealand still believes that it can stay away or at least minimize the negative impact of the geopolitical competition between the United States and China as a result of its unique geographical location in the world.

From 2008 to 2017 the National Party controlled the government and this "naïve kiwi optimism" reflected New Zealand's attitudes toward US hegemony, China's rise, and its security ties with Australia. First, although New

Zealand realized the potential power transition between the declining United States and the rising China, it did not perceive geopolitical conflict between the United States and China. The 2010 *Defence White Paper* stated that "the United States (US) is likely to remain the pre-eminent military power for the next 25 years, but its relative technological and military edge will diminish" (MoD, 2010, p. 11). In its 2016 *Defence White Paper*, however, the positive assessment of US preponderance in the region disappeared. Instead, it states that:

> By 2030 Asia is expected to have surpassed North America and Europe combined in terms of global power, a measure defined by gross domestic product, population size, military spending and technological investment. Nowhere is this shift, driven primarily by three decades of sustained economic growth in China, more striking than in North Asia. (MoD, 2016, p. 25)

It does not mean that New Zealand ignores the rising tensions during the order transition. However, it holds some "cautious optimism" because political elites of New Zealand believe that:

> [D]espite the rising tensions outlined above the likelihood of major conflict remains low. Unlike the Cold War, all states in Asia (with the exception of North Korea) are fully integrated into the global economy. This provides a powerful incentive for all regional actors to maintain a stable environment, conducive to economic growth and trade. (MoD, 2015, p. 40)

It is clear that political leaders of New Zealand firmly believe that globalization and economic interdependence will reduce the possibility of conflicts among great powers.

Second, New Zealand's political elites believe that China's rise will contribute to "regional stability and prosperity" (MoD, 2010, p. 30). The 2010 *Defence White Paper* implicitly acknowledged a rare understanding of China's "assertive diplomacy" after the GFC. It states that:

> there will be a natural tendency for it [China] to define and pursue its interests in a more forthright way on the back of growing wealth and power. The pace of China's military modernisation and force projection programme, and the response this could prompt from neighbouring states, may test the relationships of major regional powers. (MoD, 2010, p. 30)

It is true that this statement shows some worries over China's rise and its implications for regional security. However, it did not explicitly point the finger at China as a "threat" to the region. More importantly, it seemed to support the legitimate pursuits of China's rise in the region.

In the 2016 *Defence White Paper*, the New Zealand government further expressed its concerns over the complicated sovereignty and maritime disputes, especially in the South China Sea and the East China Sea. Again, it did not directly criticize any country, especially China. Rather, it states that "New Zealand supports the rights of states to seek recourse to international dispute settlement through international institutions, as well as solving disputes through direct negotiations. It is important that all states respect the final outcomes of such Processes" (MoD, 2016, p. 31). Apparently, this statement directly refers to the South China Sea arbitration between the Philippines and China. However, it did not directly target China; rather, it reiterated New Zealand's long-time policy principle on international disputes. In comparison, as discussed in the Australia section, Australia explicitly pushed China to abide by the ruling of the arbitral tribunal in its *2017 Foreign Policy White Paper*.

Last but not least, New Zealand holds strong strategic trust and security dependence on Australia, which is seen as "the most important security partner" (MoD, 2010, p. 28). Although New Zealand withdrew from its military alliance with the United States in the 1980s, it is still an official military ally of Australia. As mentioned before, geographically, Australia is a natural protector of New Zealand. Therefore, NZ's *Defence White Paper* in 2016 states that "New Zealand has no better friend and no closer ally. Through its size, location and strategic reach, Australia contributes significantly to New Zealand's security" (MoD, 2016, p. 32).

More interestingly, New Zealand seems to outsource its security to Australia to a certain degree by stating that "New Zealand's own security is enhanced by the investment which Australia has made in its national defence. Australia has military capabilities that we do not have, which are essential for higher end contingencies" (MoD, 2010, p. 18). On the one hand, this statement signifies New Zealand's strong strategic trust in the ANZAC alliance. On the other hand, it also reflects New Zealand's "naïve kiwi optimism" regarding the international order transition because it seems to be comfortable to "free ride" on Australia's defense protection by relying on Australia as an "alliance shelter" for its security (Bailes, Thayer, & Thorhallsson, 2016; Steff & Dodd-Parr, 2019).

In sum, from 2008 to 2017, policymakers in Wellington well understood that the world was experiencing a potential order transition driven by the rise of China and the relative decline of the United States. However, compared to other countries, especially Australia and Singapore in our case studies, New Zealand's isolated location causes its government to hold an optimistic and also somehow indifferent view on the international order transition, especially on China's rise. In our model, the optimistic view of order transition (benefits >

costs) places New Zealand into Cell 3 in Figure 1, suggesting a bandwagoning strategy to accommodate the rising power. The indifferent perception of the order transition due to its unique geographical location, however, puts New Zealand into Cell 4, which advocates a buck-passing policy to stay away from great power politics. Therefore, in our model New Zealand is placed between Cell 3 and Cell 4 from 2008 to 2017. It suggests that New Zealand's foreign policy under the National Party was characterized by both bandwagoning and buck-passing in the context of international order transition.

Like most countries in Asia, New Zealand has kept close economic ties with China in the post–Cold War era. To a certain extent, it could be interpreted as a bandwagoning strategy for economic profits. As Tim Groser, the former Minister of Trade (2008–2015) under the National government stated, "New Zealand has a relationship with China that no other developed country has" (Groser, 2012, cited by Young, 2017, p. 515). In the "NZ Inc. China Strategy" published in 2012, the New Zealand government proudly listed four "firsts" of its relationship with China in comparison with other Western economies, including the first country to support China's WTO admission in 1997, the first to recognize China's market economy status in 2004, the first to negotiate a Free Trade Agreement (FTA) with China in 2004, as well as the first OECD country to sign a high-quality and comprehensive FTA with China in 2008 (MFAT, 2012, p. 7).

After the 2008 GFC, New Zealand further strengthened its economic ties with China by supporting China's economic and strategic initiatives. For example, New Zealand is the first Western country that supported China's AIIB proposal in 2015. In 2017, it became the first Western economy to sign an MOU with the Chinese government to endorse China's BRI. Given the United States's negative reactions toward both AIIB and BRI, New Zealand's enthusiastic support for China's initiatives seems to be puzzling because of New Zealand's traditional security ties with the United States. However, from a perspective of the combination of bandwagoning and buck-passing strategy, it makes perfect sense. By supporting China's initiatives, New Zealand will benefit economically from China. New Zealand well recognized the potential strategic implications of China's initiatives for great power politics, especially the US–China competition. However, it might not care to deal with China directly because other countries, the United States and Australia, will carry the "bucks" or potential risks in dealing with China's initiatives and ambitions.

Therefore, besides bandwagoning with China for economic profits, New Zealand has also improved its security ties with the United States so that it could pass the "bucks" or "risks" to the United States if needed. The 2010 Wellington Declaration and the 2012 Washington Declaration were two important steps to restore defense ties between New Zealand and the United States, which were suspended because New Zealand refused to allow the US nuclear-powered warships to visit its territorial waters in the 1980s. Although New Zealand is still not in a formal alliance with the United States, the defense cooperation between the two countries improved rapidly after these two declarations. For example, the US Secretary of Defence visited New Zealand in 2012, the first visit in the past thirty years. In addition, Obama lifted restrictions on New Zealand warship's visits to US bases. It seems to signify the restoration of military cooperation between the two nations after the official split of the Australia, New Zealand, and United States Security Treaty.

It should be noted that doing business with China while seeking security from the United States is a typical hedging behavior for many countries, especially in Southeast Asia. To a certain extent, New Zealand's policy behavior appears similar to Singapore's, which can be categorized as a hedging strategy. However, given New Zealand's traditional ties with the United States and Australia as well as the strategic context of the US pivot or rebalance toward Asia after 2011, we suggest that New Zealand's restoration of security ties with the United States is more like a preparation for buck-passing than a hedging policy. There are two key differences between buck-passing and hedging. First, buck-passing is a reactive action while hedging is a proactive one. Second, the goal of buck-passing is to avoid potential risks while hedging's objective is to offset potential risks.

Despite the nuclear ship dispute in the 1980s, New Zealand shares many common identities with the United States, including the democratic political system, language, and history. More importantly, they have a common military ally – Australia. Therefore, against the background of Obama's pivot or rebalance to Asia starting in 2011, New Zealand had no choice but to improve its security ties with the United States. Just as its 2016 *Defence White Paper* states, "this strengthening [of security ties with the United States] is part of a broader United States 'rebalance' towards the Asia-Pacific region, involving greater United States diplomatic, economic and military investment in the region" (MoD, 2016, p. 32). The underlying message is that it was the United States that approached New Zealand to improve military relations.

In addition, the major purpose of restoring security ties with the United States is to fix an old problem between the two nations over the nuclear ship dispute, instead of a joint effort to cope with any future challenges, especially from China's rise. As Ayson points out, New Zealand has "limited power projection capabilities and are more suited to the lower intensity environment of the South Pacific than the mid- and higher intensity environment of the wider Asia

Pacific" (Ayson, 2012, p. 348). In other words, New Zealand is not a qualified balancer in terms of military capability for the United States in dealing with China. Therefore, it is quite difficult to argue that New Zealand's efforts to repair security relations with the United States aim to balance against China's rise. However, it is rational for New Zealand to restore a certain level of security ties with the United States so that the United States can help New Zealand to deter potential threats, that is, to take the "bucks" in the future.

In the 2017 election, the National Party was defeated by the coalition led by the Labour Party with support from the New Zealand First Party and the Green Party. Consequently, Jacinda Arden from Labour took the Prime Minister position while the New Zealand First Party held the portfolios of both Foreign Minister and Defense Minister. Compared to the National Party, political leaders from the New Zealand First Party, especially Winston Peters (foreign minister) and Ron Mark (defense minister), held more alarming views on China's rise, which were reflected in the 2018 Strategic Defence Policy Statement (SDPS). For example, the SDPS listed "three forces pressuring on the international order," including great powers' "pursuit of sphere of influence," "challenges to the open society," and "complex disrupters" (MoD, 2018, pp. 16–20). China was singled out as a major actor of the first force threatening the international order because "China has not consistently adopted the governance and values championed by the order's traditional leaders. Both domestically and as a basis for international engagement, China holds views on human rights and freedom of information that stand in contrast to those that prevail in New Zealand" (MoD, 2018, p. 17). The 2018 SDPS clearly, for the first time, criticized China's declaration of the Air Defence Identification Zone in the East China Sea in 2013 as well as China's land reclamations in the South China Sea. Moreover, it alerted to China's increasing influence in the South Pacific, New Zealand's traditional sphere of influence (Capie, 2019; Ayson, 2020a).

Just because of the increasingly negative views of the New Zealand government on China's rise under the strong influence of the First Party, New Zealand's previous cost-and-benefit calculation regarding the international order transition also moved dramatically. The costs for the potential change in the international order increase while the benefits from the change decrease. Therefore, in our model illustrated by Figure 1, New Zealand moves to Cell 2, inclining to a balancing policy toward the rising power – the driver of the international order transition. Consequently, after 2018 we witnessed some policy shifts of New Zealand from a "bandwagoning-and-buck-passing" direction to a "balancing" direction. For example, New Zealand launched its "Pacific reset" policy to countervail China's increasing influence in the Pacific by cooperating with Australia and the United States (Capie, 2019; Ayson, 2020a). In addition, New Zealand upgraded some of its military equipment with the purchase of P-8 and C130 Js in order to reinforce its military interoperability with Australia and the United States (Capie, 2019). Following the other Five Eyes countries, New Zealand also banned Huawei's participation in the 5G infrastructure projects although it used a "technical" reason instead of the national security excuse (Gee & Patman, 2021).

It is worth noting that Labor Prime Minister Ardern seemed to have different views on China as well as on geopolitical competition from New Zealand First leaders Peters and Mark, who controlled both foreign and defense minister portfolios in the coalition government in 2017–2020 (Ayson, 2020b). Therefore, we see some policy discrepancies between the Prime Minister on the one hand and the Foreign and Defence ministers on the other. For example, while Foreign Minister Peters raised some concerns on New Zealand's support for China's BRI, Prime Minister Ardern confirmed New Zealand's endorsement of the BRI during her visit to Beijing in April 2019.

After the Labor Party won the 2019 election with the majority in the parliament, Ardern removed Peters and Mark from the cabinet in 2020. Although emphasizing a value-based foreign policy, Ardern seemingly had less appetite for geopolitics (Ayson, 2020b). Consequently, New Zealand started to return to the previous foreign policy strategy combining bandwagoning with buck-passing in the context of US–China competition. In early 2020, New Zealand upgraded its FTA with China despite Australia – its closest ally – being involved in a trade war with China. It is reported that New Zealand's trade minister even suggested that Australia should pay some "respect" to China in order to avoid the consequence of the trade war (Dziedzic, 2021).

New Zealand's "buck-passing" attitudes are also reflected in its policies on some sensitive issues related to China in that New Zealand seems reluctant to challenge China directly with other "Five Eyes" countries. For example, in March 2021, New Zealand welcomed the measures announced by Canada, the EU, the United Kingdom, and the United States against China over the Xinjiang issue, but it did not join in the travel bans and asset freezes of specified officials or the Xinjiang products. Regarding Australia's proposal to make the Five Eyes an economic cooperation group, New Zealand's response in 2020 was lukewarm at best. In early 2021, New Zealand's foreign minister, Nanaia Mahuta, publicly refuted efforts by Australia to pressure China through the Five Eyes intelligence-sharing group. As Mahuta states, the idea of expanding the diplomatic architecture really exists "outside the remit of the Five Eyes," which should focus on intelligence sharing (Dziedzic, 2021). Moreover, Mahuta compared the relationship between China and New Zealand to a dragon and taniwha (a water-dwelling serpent in Maori mythology), highlighting the mutual respect with China (Young, 2021). After the outbreak of the Ukrainian War, Australia and the United Kingdom warned that Russia's invasion of Ukraine had a direct parallel with China's intentions for Taiwan. Arden, however, publicly declined to make a similar comparison, stating that diplomacy and dialogue were the key to preventing conflict across the Taiwan strait (Bourke, 2022).

Compared to Australia's confrontational stand against China in recent years, New Zealand's policy toward China is indeed different and puzzling. Some suggest that it is rooted in New Zealand's "small trading country" identity, which has different perceptions of "ontological security" (Young, 2017). Others argue that as a small country, New Zealand holds a different strategic outlook and is more likely to be influenced by domestic politics in foreign policy than a large power (Köllner, 2021). All these arguments reveal some elements of truth in explaining New Zealand's foreign policy. Our research, however, suggests that New Zealand's foreign policy orientation is mainly shaped by its policymakers' perceptions regarding the costs and benefits from the potential order transition. Since the Ardern administration under the Labor Party is less interested in geopolitics due to its unique geographical location in the world (Ayson, 2020b), a buck-passing strategy is a rational policy choice for New Zealand to avoid the risks from the international order transition. However, successful buck-passing will not be easy because the "buck bearer," either the United States or Australia, might not want to take the "bucks" or risks for New Zealand. Prime Minister Jacinda Ardern announced her resignation in late 2022. How will domestic political dynamics influence New Zealand's political elites' perceptions of the future order transition? How will the changing perceptions and preferences shape New Zealand's policy choices between the United States and China? These questions are worth investigating in the future.

Conclusion

This project introduces a "preference-for-change" model to shed some light on secondary states' policy choices in the context of international order transition. It argues that political leaders' cost-and-benefit perceptions regarding the order transition shape a state's policy choices among four strategies: hedging, balancing, bandwagoning, and buck-passing. The ambiguous cost–benefit perception of the order transition has led Singapore to adopt a hedging strategy to bet on both sides – the United States and China. The negative views on the order transition and China's rise, especially since 2016–2017, have encouraged Australia to balance against China in various ways.

The positive perceptions of China's rise and negative views on United States interference in internal affairs, however, have driven Thai leaders to prefer the China-led order transition to the US-dominated status quo. Therefore, Thailand has conducted a bandwagoning strategy to seek profits from the rise of China and the potential order transition. Due to its uniquely isolated geographical location, New Zealand leaders have kept the "naïve kiwi optimism," in which they hold positive views about potential benefits, but indifferent views on possible costs regarding the international order transition. Consequently, New Zealand has adopted a combination of bandwagoning and buck-passing strategies so that it can do business as usual with China whilst trying to stay away from the strategic competition between the United States and China if possible. However, we also show that the changing perceptions of the order transition and China's rise by the New Zealand First Party leaders moved New Zealand's policy toward the direction of balancing against China in 2017–2019.

This preference-for-change model can be applied to explain state behavior during the period of international order transition beyond these four cases. For example, South Korea is another critical treaty ally of the United States in Asia. Like Australia, South Korean leaders also view the United States as the key security protector, especially against aggressive North Korea. However, as Jae Jeok Park (2023) points out, South Korea seems to have a more positive perception of the United States and US-led alliance in the future order transition. In the eyes of South Korean leaders, the strategic competition between the United States and China has been transformed into one between a US-led network and China, in which the US-led network or alliance will be strengthened. Moreover, China is the largest trading partner of South Korea. Because of North Korea, China is not seen as the most dangerous security threat by South Korea. Therefore, in South Korea's newly released Indo-Pacific strategy document, "Strategy for a Free, Peaceful, and Prosperous Indo-Pacific Region," in late 2022, China was called a "key partner," and South Korea said that it "will nurture a sounder and more mature relationship as we pursue shared interests based on mutual respect and reciprocity, guided by international norms and rules" (Cha, 2022).

Applying our preference-for-change model, South Korea could be located in either Cell 3 (with high-economic benefits and low-security costs) or Cell 1 (with high-economic benefits and high-security costs), or between these two cells because conservative political elites are more likely to hold a high-security alert on China than progressive politicians. According to our model, South Korea should adopt a strategy between hedging and bandwagoning. In a comprehensive study on South Korea's policy toward the United States and China from 2013 to 2019, Victor Cha (2020, p. 531) suggests that "when faced with a decision point on an issue upon which the United States and China disagree, Seoul took a position approximating more consensus with the Chinese rather than with its traditional ally." While Cha coins South Korea's behavior as an instance of "decoupling" from the United States, it is closer to bandwagoning in our preference-for-change model. However, in April 2023, South Korean President Yoon Suk-yeol made a high-profile visit to Washington D.C. during which the United States announced the deployment of a nuclear-armed submarine as a deterrent against North Korea. This development raises some concerns or uncertainties regarding South Korea's traditional approach of hedging or bandwagoning with regard to its policy towards China in the future.

Another example can be drawn from Indonesia, the largest Muslim country in the world and *de facto* leader of ASEAN. Similar to Singapore, Indonesian leaders hold a mixed view on the rise of China and the potential decline of the United States during the period of order transition. On the one hand, it perceives that "the shift in the center of economic gravity to Asia, marked by the rise of China ... as a welcome phenomenon that can benefit its own economic development." On the other, Indonesia holds deep concerns over "China's assertiveness in pursuing its claims over the whole of the South China Sea, as well as the re-emergence of major power rivalry, particularly between the United States and China as the incumbent and ascending superpower respectively, which can disrupt regional stability and prosperity" (Anwar, 2023, p. 351). Therefore, in Indonesian Defense Minister Prabowo Subianto's words, "we (Indonesia) recognize the interests of the US as one of the preeminent powers ranging across the hemispheres ... we [also] recognize Beijing's legitimate core interests, and we support and respect Beijing's rightful place as a great world power" (cited in Anwar, 2023, p. 359).

According to our preference-for-change model, Indonesia can be placed in Cell 1 (high benefits and high costs), suggesting that Indonesia is more likely to adopt a hedging strategy between the United States and China. In reality, Indonesia has chosen a "hedging plus" strategy, not only adhering to the non-alignment tradition between the United States and China but also proactively "promoting ASEAN-centric inclusive and cooperative wider East Asian multilateralism" in order to ensure both its strategic autonomy and agency in the region (Anwar, 2023, p.351).

This preference-for-change model can also explain foreign policy behavior of states beyond the Indo-Pacific region. For example, the United Kingdom is not a traditional Indo-Pacific country but has adopted a "tilting" strategy toward the Indo-Pacific. One substantive move is to establish AUKUS – a security pact with Australia and the United States through which it will work with the United States to help Australia build its nuclear submarine fleet in 2021. According to

Shaun Breslin and Peter Burnham (2023), the United Kingdom policy shift toward the Indo-Pacific is largely shaped by "a changing dominant narrative on China and in particular by perceptions of China as a 'systemic competitor' in the global political economy" (Breslin & Burnham, 2023, p. 406). Therefore, in our preference-for-change model, we can place the United Kingdom in cell 2, like Australia, because of its high-cost and low-benefit perception regarding the potential order transition between the United States and China. The United Kingdom's "tilting" toward the Indo-Pacific policy is a "balancing" behavior through which the United Kingdom has taken sides with the United States to defend the existing order and resist the potential change driven by China's rise.

Scholars are encouraged to apply this preference-for-change model to make sense of states' policy choices against the background of US–China strategic competition. However, a related and legitimate question is: why do political leaders hold different perceptions of the order transition? This question is beyond the scope of this study but worth further research. Leaders' cognitive perceptions are influenced by many factors, such as ideology, personality, domestic politics, and the international environment. Our preference-for-change model does not deny the complexity of different countries' decision-making processes. Nor does it refute the role of various domestic and ideational variables, such as regime type, ideology, nationalism, and even emotion in shaping political leaders' perceptions as well as their policy choices during the period of international order transition.

For example, ideology has played an important role in shaping leaders' perceptions in Australia and New Zealand. In both countries, conservative political leaders are more likely to hold a strong and positive view of the current liberal international order led by the United States. In contrast, liberal or progressive leaders seem to be open to embracing the economic opportunities brought by China's rise. Therefore, after the Australian Labor Party won the general election in late May 2022, Australia started to engage in repairing its damaged relations with China. However, it is still too early to predict that Australia will change its "balancing" policy choice, that is, to support the United States against the potential change driven by China, during the period of order transition. Other factors, including China's policy behavior and US influence, might also shape Australia's public opinions as well as leaders' perceptions regarding China's rise and potential United States decline in the future international order. In the 2022 public opinion survey by the Lowy Institute, about one in ten (12 percent) respondents "trust" China, a forty-point decrease since 2018. In comparison, trust in the United States was stable at 65 percent (Kassam, 2022). How Australia's public opinion influences political elites' perceptions of and preference for the potential order transition in the context of the US–China strategic competition will be an exciting topic for scholars to pursue in the future.

For non-democratic systems, the Thailand case suggests that the domestic political concern over regime security is the major reason for policy elites to adopt a favorable view of China's rise as well as the related order transition because China seems to be more inclined to the non-interference principle than the United States. To a certain extent, sovereignty and nationalism, these ideational variables, have played an important role in shaping Thai leaders' perceptions of the potential order transition driven by the US–China strategic competition. The regime-type oriented hypothesis might offer some policy insights to US leaders on how to cope with non-democratic regimes in the strategic competition with China.

Our neoclassical realist model does consider leaders' perceptions as a domestic transmission belt linking the international system and states' policy choices. However, since neoclassical realism assumes that leaders are rational in making decisions under the anarchic international system, our rational-choice-based, parsimonious model, focuses on the cost–benefit calculation of leaders regarding the potential order transition in the system. It does not deny that various material, cognitive, emotional, and ideational variables might change and influence leaders' perceptions and preferences beyond mere cost–benefit calculations. However, we argue that our preference-for-change model can provide a "first-cut" explanation of the general trends of a state's policy choice during the period of order transition.[11] Other scholars are encouraged to test this "preference-for-change" model as well as address its deficiencies by identifying domestic causal mechanisms, and by providing more detailed "second-cut" explanations of a state's foreign policy decisions during the international order transition.

It is worth noting that our dependent variable of the "preference-for-change" model is states' foreign policy behaviors, not international politics. As we have explained, our neoclassical realist model follows the type I and type II approaches in neoclassical realism, in which our research focuses on states' foreign policy choices instead of the outcomes of state interaction, that is, international politics. Inspired by the efforts of type III neoclassical realists (Ripsman, Taliaferro, & Lobell, 2016), we can preliminarily explore the structural implications of the "preference-for-change" model for international order transition in the international system as well as international politics in general.

First, leaders' perceptions of international order transition matter. If more states prefer an order transition led by China's rise, a bandwagoning strategy

---

[11] For the division of labor between first-cut and second-cut theorizations, see Keohane (1986).

will become a popular policy choice in the system, through which more states will work with China to push for the order transition in the system. However, if more states intend to keep the existing international order in which they benefit from US leadership, a balancing policy will become a dominant strategy for secondary powers in the region. How to influence and shape the perceptions of secondary states will be a key strategic question for policymakers in the United States and China to consider during their strategic competition. Besides material interests, such as offering public goods to woo regional powers, they should also elaborate on how to play the cultural, ideological, and ideational cards to win the hearts and minds of local people and societies because all politicians and political elites will need to be responsive and responsible for their constituencies to various degrees, no matter whether in democracies or autocracies. To a certain extent, the strategic competition between the United States and China is not only about material power and domination but also about values and ideas.

Second, the nature of the international order transition, either peaceful or not, will be largely shaped by the US–China strategic interactions. How the United States and China behave as well as compete with one another will shape the perceptions of these secondary powers and, more importantly, the potential outcome of international order transition. To a certain extent, this finding vindicates Type III neoclassical realism, suggesting that we can somehow rely on examining grand strategies of great powers to expand the explanatory domain of neoclassical realism from foreign policy to international politics (Ripsman, Taliaferro, & Lobell, 2016). Although the strategic competition between the United States and China is inevitable, how they will compete with one another matters. If they choose a violent approach to either overthrow or defend the international order, they will certainly fall into the "Thucydides trap," leaving other countries with a tough and tragic choice. However, if they behave in a constructive way and compete in a peaceful manner, it will leave more room for other states to hedge between the two. In an ideal situation of benign and healthy competition between the United States and China, secondary states can still choose a hedging strategy by actively balancing their relations between the two giants. Moreover, secondary states can even play a positive role in alleviating the strategic tension between the United States and China if they can coordinate their "hedging" efforts. The world is changing, and states are at a crossroads in making decisions. Hedging is not dying. It largely depends on how the United States and China compete with one another during the period of international order transition. The current status of US–China competition, however, suggests that we might have entered the "after-hedging" era.

References

Acharya, A. (2008). *Singapore's Foreign Policy: The Search for Regional Order*. Singapore: World Scientific.

Alagappa, M. (2003). The study of international order: An analytical framework. In M. Alagappa, ed., *Asian Security Order: Instrumental and Normative Features*. Stanford: Stanford University Press, pp. 33–69.

Allison, G. (2017). *Destined for War: Can America and China Escape Thucydides's Trap?* Boston: Houghton Mifflin Harcourt.

Almond, G., & Genco, S. J. (1977). Clouds, clocks, and the study of politics. *World Politics*, **29**(4), 489–522.

Anwar, D. F. (2023). Indonesia's hedging plus policy in the face of China's rise and the US-China rivalry in the Indo-Pacific region. *The Pacific Review*, **36** (2), 351–377. https://doi.org/10.1080/09512748.2022.2160794.

Art, R. J. (2004). Europe hedges its security bets. In T. V. Paul, J. J. Wirtz, & M. Fortmann, eds., *Balance of Power: Theory and Practice in the 21st Century*. Stanford: Stanford University Press, pp. 179–213.

Ayson, R. (2012). Choosing ahead of time?: Australia, New Zealand and the US-China contest in Asia. *Contemporary Southeast Asia: A Journal of International and Strategic Affairs*, **34**(3), 338–64.

Ayson, R. (2020a). New Zealand and the great irresponsibles: Coping with Russia, China and the US. *Australian Journal of International Affairs*, **74**(4), 455–78.

Ayson, R. (2020b). New Zealand: A re-elected government with less appetite for geopolitics. In R. Huisken, &K. Brett, eds., *CSCAP Regional Security Outlook 2021*. Report, Council for Security Cooperation in the Asia Pacific: Wellington, pp. 52–54.

Ba, A. D. (2019). China's "Belt and Road" in Southeast Asia: Constructing the strategic narrative in Singapore. *Asian Perspective*, **43**(2), 249–72.

Bagshaw, E., & Harris, T. (September 24, 2019). China claims Australia the "pioneer" of a global anti-China campaign. *The Sydney Morning Herald*. www.smh.com.au/politics/federal/china-claims-australia-the-pioneer-of-a-global-anti-china-campaign-20190924-p52ufk.html.

Bailes, A. J. K., Thayer, B. A., & Thorhallsson, B. (2016). Alliance theory and alliance "shelter": The complexities of small state alliance behaviour. *Third World Thematics: A TWQ Journal*, **1**(1), 9–26.

Baldino, D., & Carr, A. (February 26, 2016). The end of 2%: Australia gets serious about its defence budget. *The Conversation*. https://theconversation.com/the-end-of-2-australia-gets-serious-about-its-defence-budget-53554.

Biden, J. (May 23, 2022). Remarks by President Biden at Indo-Pacific Economic Framework for Prosperity Launch Event. Tokyo, Japan: Izumi Garden Gallery. www.whitehouse.gov/briefing-room/speeches-remarks/ 2022/05/23/remarks-by-president-biden-at-indo-pacific-economic-frame work-for-prosperity-launch-event/.

Bishop, J. (March 13, 2017). Change and uncertainty in the Indo-Pacific: Strategic challenges and opportunities. *28th IISS Fullerton Lecture*. www .foreignminister.gov.au/minister/julie-bishop/speech/change-and-uncer tainty-indo-pacific-strategic-challenges-and-opportunities.

Bisley, N. (2017). Australia and the evolving international order. In M. Beeson & S. Hameiri, eds., *Navigating the New International Disorder: Australia in the World Affairs, 2011–2015*. Oxford: Oxford University Press, pp. 39–55.

Bisley, N. (July 27, 2018). Australia's rules based international order. Speech at the Australian Institute of International Affairs (AIIA). www.internationalaf fairs.org.au/australianoutlook/australias-rules-based-international-order/.

Bisley, N., & Schreer, B. (2018). Australia and the rules-based order in Asia: Of principles and pragmatism. *Asian Survey*, **58**(2), 302–19.

Blaxland, J., & Raymond, G. (2017). *Tipping the Balance in Southeast Asia? Thailand, the United States and China*. Report, Strategic & Defence Studies Centre at the Australian National University and Center for Strategic and International Studies (CSIS), Canberra.

Bourke, L. (July 2, 2022). "Diplomacy, diplomacy, diplomacy": Ardern on preventing Chinese takeover of Taiwan. *The Sydney Morning Herald*. www.smh.com.au/world/oceania/diplomacy-diplomacy-diplomacy-ardern- s-solution-for-preventing-chinese-takeover-of-taiwan-20220702-p5ayi3 .html.

Bradsher, K. (March 7, 2023). China's leader, with rare bluntness, blames U.S. containment for troubles. *The New York Times*. www.nytimes.com/ 2023/03/07/world/asia/china-us-xi-jinping.html.

Breslin, S., & Burnham, P. (2023). International order transition and the UK's tilt to the "Indo-Pacific." *The Pacific Review*, **36** (2), 406–32. https://doi.org/ 10.1080/09512748.2022.2160796.

Bull, H. (1977). *The Anarchical Society: A Study of Order in World Politics*. New York: Macmillan.

Busbarat, P. (2016). "Bamboo swirling in the wind": Thailand's foreign policy imbalance between China and the United States. *Contemporary Southeast Asia*, **38**(2), 233–57.

Busbarat, P. (2017). Thai–US relations in the post-cold war era: Untying the special relationship. *Asian Security*, **13**(3), 256–74.

Busbarat, P. (2019). Thailand's foreign policy towards neighbouring countries and ASEAN. In P. Chachavalpongpun, ed., *Routledge Handbook of Contemporary Thailand*. London: Routledge, pp. 431–46.

Capie, D. (2019). The regional security outlook: A New Zealand perspective. In R. Huisken, & K. Brett, eds., *CSCAP Regional Security Outlook + ARF – The Next 25 Years 2019 Council for Security Cooperation in the Asia Pacific*. Report, Council for Security Cooperation in the Asia Pacific, pp. 45–47.

Catalinac, A. L. (2010). Why New Zealand took itself out of ANZUS: Observing "opposition for autonomy" in asymmetric alliances. *Foreign Policy Analysis*, **6**(4), 317–38.

Cha, S. (December 28, 2023). South Korea barely mentions China in new Indo-Pacific strategy. *Bloomberg*. www.bloomberg.com/news/articles/2022-12-28/south-korea-barely-mentions-china-in-new-indo-pacific-strategy.

Cha, V. D. (2018). *Powerplay: The Origins of the American Alliance System in Asia*, vol. 151. Princeton: Princeton University Press.

Cha, V. D. (2020). Allied decoupling in an era of US–China strategic competition. *The Chinese Journal of International Politics*, **13**(4), 509–36.

Chan, I. (2019). Reversing China's Belt-and-Road initiative – Singapore's response to the BRI and its quest for relevance. *East Asia*, **36**(3), 185–204.

Chan, L. H. (2020). Strategic hedging. *Asia Policy*, **15**(3), 87–112.

Chan, S., Feng, H., He, K., & Hu, W. (2021). *Contesting Revisionism: The United States, China, and Transformation of International Order*. Oxford: Oxford University Press.

Chong, J. I. (April 26, 2017). Diverging paths? Singapore-China relations and the East Asian maritime domain. *Maritime Awareness Project*. www.nbr.org/publication/diverging-paths-singapore-china-relations-and-the-east-asian-maritime-domain/.

Chongkittavorn, K. (April 13, 2015). Relations with major powers shake-up status quo. *The Nation*. www.nationthailand.com/perspective/30257955.

Choong, W. (July 14, 2021). Chinese-U.S. split is forcing Singapore to choose sides. *Foreign Policy*. https://foreignpolicy.com/2021/07/14/singapore-china-us-southeast-asia-asean-geopolitics/.

Chow, J. (June 3, 2016). US has "no better friend than Singapore" in the region, says Defence Secretary Carter, *The Straits Times*. www.straitstimes.com/singapore/us-has-no-better-friend-than-singapore-in-the-region-defence-secretary-carter.

Christensen, T. J. (1996). *Useful Adversaries: Grand Strategy, Domestic Mobilization, and Sino-American Conflict, 1947–1958*, vol. 179. Princeton: Princeton University Press.

Christensen, T. J. (March 24, 2021). There will not be a new cold war: The limits of U.S.-Chinese competition. *Foreign Affairs*. www.foreignaffairs.com/art icles/united-states/2021-03-24/there-will-not-be-new-cold-war.

Christensen, T. J., & Snyder, J. (1990). Chain gangs and passed bucks: Predicting alliance patterns in multipolarity. *International Organization*, **44**(2), 137–68.

Ciorciari, J. D. (2019). The variable effectiveness of hedging strategies. *International Relations of the Asia-Pacific*, **19**(3), 523–55.

Ciorciari, J. D., & Haacke, J. (2019). Hedging in international relations: An introduction. *International Relations of the Asia-Pacific*, **19**(3), 367–74.

Cogan, M. S. (2019). Is Thailand accommodating China? *Southeast Asian Social Science Review*, **4**(2), 24–47.

Davidson, H. (April 29, 2020). Chewing gum stuck on the sole of our shoes: The China-Australia war of words – timeline. *The Guardian*. www.theguardian .com/world/2020/apr/29/chewing-gum-stuck-on-the-sole-of-our-shoes-the-china-australia-war-of-words-timeline.

Department of Defence, Australia (DoD). (2009). *Defence White Paper 2009*. Canberra: Australian Government.

Department of Defence, Australia (DoD). (2013). *Defence White Paper 2013*. Canberra: Australian Government.

Department of Defence, Australia (DoD). (2016). *Defence White Paper 2016*. Canberra: Australian Government.

Department of Defence, Australia (DoD). (2020). *Strategic Update 2020*. Canberra: Australian Government.

Department of Foreign Affairs and Trade, Australia (DFAT). (2017). *2017 Foreign Policy White Paper*. Canberra: Australian Government.

Dziedzic, S. (April 19, 2021). New Zealand "uncomfortable with expanding the remit" of Five Eyes, says Foreign Minister. *ABC News*. www.abc.net.au/ news/2021-04-19/new-zealand-five-eyes-intelligence-sharing-china-austra lia/100078834.

Eckstein, H. (1975). Case study and theory in political science. In F. I. Greenstein, & N. W. Polsby, eds., *Handbook of Political Science, vol. 7: Strategies of Inquiry*. Reading: Addison-Wesley, pp. 79–133.

Elman, C. (1996). Horses for courses: Why nor neorealist theories of foreign policy? *Security Studies*, **6**(1), 7–53.

Emmerson, D. K. (2018). China in Xi's "new era": Singapore and Goliath? *Journal of Democracy*, **29**(2), 76–82.

English, B. (June 23, 2017). Speech to NZ Institute of International Affairs. www.beehive.govt.nz/speech/speech-nz-institute-international-affairs-2.

Feng, H., & He, K. eds. (2020). *China's Challenges and International Order Transition: Beyond the "Thucydides Trap."* Ann Arbor: University of Michigan Press.

Foot, R. (2006). Chinese strategies in a US-hegemonic global order: Accommodating and hedging. *International affairs*, **82**(1), 77–94.

Foot, R., & Goh, E. (2019). The international relations of East Asia: A new research prospectus. *International Studies Review*, **21**(3), 398–423.

Fuller, T. (December 8, 2011). U.S. citizen sentenced for insulting Thai King. *The New York Times*. www.nytimes.com/2011/12/09/world/asia/us-citizen-sentenced-for-insulting-thai-king.html.

Ganesan, N. (2005). *Realism and Interdependence in Singapore's Foreign Policy*. London: Routledge.

Gee, A., & Patman, R. G. (2021). Small state or minor power? New Zealand's Five Eyes membership, intelligence reforms, and Wellington's response to China's growing Pacific role. *Intelligence and National Security*, **36**(1), 34–50.

George, A. L., & Bennett, A. (2004). *Case Studies and Theory Development in the Social Sciences*. Cambridge, MA: MIT Press.

Gilpin, R. (1981). *War and Change in World Politics*. Cambridge: Cambridge University Press.

Glaser, C. L. (1997). The security dilemma revisited. *World Politics*, **50**(1), 171–201.

Glaser, C. L. (2010). *Rational Theory of International Politics*. Princeton: Princeton University Press.

Glaser, C. L. (2019). A flawed framework: Why the liberal international order concept is misguided. *International Security*, **43**(4), 51–87.

Goh, E. (August 31, 2006). Understanding "hedging" in Asia-Pacific security. *PacNet*, **43**. www.csis-website-prod.s3.amazonaws.com/s3fs-public/legacy_files/files/media/csis/pubs/pac0643.pdf

Goh, E. (2007). Great powers and hierarchical order in Southeast Asia: Analyzing regional security strategies. *International Security*, **32**(3), 113–57.

Gong, X. (2019). The belt & road initiative and China's influence in Southeast Asia. *The Pacific Review*, **32**(4), 635–65.

Groser, T. (April 28, 2012) The nation – Tim Groser: transcript, Scoop. www.business.scoop.co.nz/2012/04/28/the-nation-tim-groser-transcript.

Gyngell, A. (2019). History hasn't ended: How to handle China. *Australian Foreign Affairs*, **7**, 5–27.

Haacke, J. (2019). The concept of hedging and its application to Southeast Asia: A critique and a proposal for a modified conceptual and methodological framework. *International Relations of the Asia-Pacific*, **19**(3), 375–417.

Haass, R. (April 7, 2020). The pandemic will accelerate history rather than reshape it. *Foreign Affairs*. www.foreignaffairs.com/articles/united-states/2020-04-07/pandemic-will-accelerate-history-rather-reshape-it.

Han, E. (2018). Under the shadow of China-US competition: Myanmar and Thailand's alignment choices. *The Chinese Journal of International Politics*, **11**(1), 81–104.

He, K. (2008). Institutional balancing and international relations theory: Economic interdependence and balance of power strategies in Southeast Asia. *European Journal of International Relations*, **14**(3), 489–518.

He, K. (2009). *Institutional Balancing in the Asia-Pacific: Economic Interdependence and China's Rise*. London: Routledge.

He, K. (2016). China's Crisis Behavior. Cambridge: Cambridge University Press.

He, K. (2019). Contested Multilateralism 2.0 and regional order transition: Causes and implications. *The Pacific Review*, **32**(2), 210–20.

He, K., ed. (2020). *Contested Multilateralism 2.0 and Asian Security Dynamics*. London: Routledge.

He, K., & Chan, S. (2018). Thinking about change: American theorizing and Chinese reasoning on world politics. *International Studies Review*, **20**(2), 326–33.

He, K., & Feng, H. (2008). If not soft balancing, then what? Reconsidering soft balancing and US policy toward China. *Security Studies*, **17**(2), 363–95.

He, K., & Feng, H. (2020). Introduction: Rethinking China and international order: A conceptual analysis. In H. Feng, & K. He, eds., *China's Challenges and International Order Transition: Beyond "Thucydides's Trap."* Ann Arbor: University of Michigan Press, pp. 1–24.

He, K., & Feng, H. (2023). International order transition and US-China strategic competition in the Indo Pacific. *The Pacific Review*, **36** (2), 234–60. https://doi.org/10.1080/09512748.2022.2160789.

He, K., Feng, H., Chan, S., & Hu, W. (2021). Rethinking revisionism in world politics. *The Chinese Journal of International Politics*, **14**(2), 159–86.

Hewison, K. (2018). Thailand: An old relationship renewed. *The Pacific Review*, **31**(1), 116–30.

Hurst, D. (September 15, 2020). Australia criticises China over treatment of Uighurs and for eroding freedoms in Hong Kong. *The Guardian*. www.theguardian.com/australia-news/2020/sep/15/australia-criticises-china-over-treatment-of-uighurs-and-for-eroding-freedoms-in-hong-kong.

Ikenberry, G. J. (2008). The rise of China and the future of the West: Can the liberal system survive? *Foreign Affairs*, **87**(1), 23–56.

Ikenberry, G. J. (2016). Between the eagle and the dragon: America, China, and middle state strategies in East Asia. *Political Science Quarterly*, **131**(1), 9–43.

Ikenberry, G. J. (2017). The rise, character, and evolution of international order. In O. Fioretos, ed., *International Politics and Institutions in Time*. Oxford: Oxford University Press, pp. 59–75.

Ikenberry, G. J. (2018). The end of liberal international order? *International Affairs*, **94**(1), 7–23.

Jackson, V. (2014). Power, trust, and network complexity: Three logics of hedging in Asian security. *International Relations of the Asia-Pacific*, **14**(3), 331–56.

Jervis, R. (1998). *System Effects: Complexity in Political and Social Life*. Princeton: Princeton University Press.

Johnston, A. I. (2014). *Social States: China in International Institutions, 1980–2000*. Princeton: Princeton University Press.

Jones, D. M., & Jenne, N. (2021). Hedging and grand strategy in Southeast Asian foreign policy. *International Relations of the Asia-Pacific*, **22**(2), 205–35.

Kang, D. C. (2003). Getting Asia wrong: The need for new analytical frameworks. *International Security*, **27**(4), 57–85.

Kang, D. C. (2007). *China Rising: Peace, Power, and Order in East Asia*. New York: Columbia University Press.

Kassam, N. (June 29, 2022). Relations with the US and China. *Lowy Institute Poll*. www.poll.lowyinstitute.org/report/2022/.

Keohane, R. (1986). Theory of world politics: Structural realism and beyond. In R. Keohane, ed., *Neorealism and its Critics*. New York: Columbia University Press, pp. 158–203.

Khong, Y. F. (1999). Singapore: A time for economic and political engagement. In A. I. Johnston, & R. S. Ross, eds., *Engaging China: The Management of an Emerging Power*. London: Routledge, pp. 109–28.

Kislenko, A. (2002). Bending with the wind: The continuity and flexibility of Thai foreign policy. *International Journal*, **57**(4), 537–61.

Kissinger, H. (April 3, 2020). The Coronavirus pandemic will forever alter the world order. *Wall Street Journal*. www.wsj.com/articles/the-coronavirus-pandemic-will-forever-alter-the-world-order-11585953005.

Köllner, P. (2021). Australia and New Zealand recalibrate their China policies: Convergence and divergence. *The Pacific Review*, **34**(3), 405–36.

Korolev, A. (2019). Shrinking room for hedging: System-unit dynamics and behavior of smaller powers. *International Relations of the Asia-Pacific*, **19**(3), 419–52.

Krauthammer, C. (1990). The unipolar moment. *Foreign Affairs*, **70**(1), 23–33.

Kuik, C.-C. (2008). The essence of hedging: Malaysia and Singapore's response to a rising China. *Contemporary Southeast Asia: A Journal of International and Strategic Affairs*, **30**(2), 159–85.

Kuik, C.-C. (2016). How do weaker states hedge? Unpacking ASEAN states' alignment behavior towards China. *Journal of Contemporary China*, **25**(100), 500–14.

Kynge, J., Manson, K., & Politi, J. (May 9, 2020). US and China: Edging towards a new type of cold war? *Financial Times*. www.ft.com/content/fe59abf8-cbb8-4931-b224-56030586fb9a.

Lake, D., Martin, L., & Risse, T. (2021). Challenges to the liberal order: Reflections on international organization. *International Organization*, **75**(2), 225–57.

Lam, P. E. (2020). Singapore in 2019. *Asian Survey*, **60**(1), 152–58.

Layne, C. (2013). The real post-American world: The Pax America's end and the future of world politics. In S. Clarke, & S. Hoque, eds., *Debating a Post-American World: What Lies Ahead*. London: Routledge, pp. 69–74.

Lee, H. L. (November 3, 2009). Excerpts from the media conference by Prime Minister Lee Hsien Loong, Chair of the 17th APEC Economic Leaders Meeting. www.pmo.gov.sg/Newsroom/excerpts-media-conference-prime-minister-lee-hsien-loong-chair-17th-apec-economic.

Lee, H. L. (April 15, 2010). Prime Minister Lee Hsien Loong's Address to Chicago Council of Global Affairs (CCGA). www.pmo.gov.sg/Newsroom/prime-minister-lee-hsien-loongs-address-chicago-council-global-affairs-ccga-15-april.

Lee, H. L. (May 29, 2015). Keynote speech by Prime Minister Lee Hsien Loong at the Shangri-La Dialogue. www.pmo.gov.sg/Newsroom/transcript-key note-speech-prime-minister-lee-hsien-loong-shangri-la-dialogue-29-may-2015.

Lee, H. L. (2020). The endangered Asian century. *Foreign Affairs*, **99**(4), 52–64.

Lee, K. Y. (April 9, 2009). The fundamentals of Singapore's foreign policy: Then and now. Speech at the S. Rajaratnam Lecture, 5:30 pm at Shangri-La Hotel, Singapore. www.pmo.gov.sg/Newsroom/speech-mr-lee-kuan-yew-minister-mentor-s-rajaratnam-lecture-09-april-2009-530-pm-shangri.

Lee, Y. N. (February 21, 2021). Biden may face an uphill task trying to form an "Anti-China Alliance" in Asia. *CNBC News*. www.cnbc.com/2021/02/22/biden-could-have-a-hard-time-gathering-asian-countries-against-china.html.

Legro, J. W. (2005). *Rethinking the World: Great Power Strategies and International Order*. Ithaca: Cornell University Press.

Legro, J. W., & Moravcsik, A. (1999). Is anyone still a realist? *International Security*, **24**(2), 5–55.

Leifer, M. (2000). *Singapore Foreign Policy: Coping with Vulnerability.* London: Routledge.

Levy, J. S. (2013). Psychology and foreign policy decision-making. In L. Huddy, D. O. Sears, & J. S. Levy, eds., *The Oxford Handbook of Political Psychology*, 2nd ed. Oxford: Oxford University Press, pp. 301–33.

Lieberthal, K., & Wang, J. (March, 2012). *Addressing US–China Strategic Distrust.* Report, John L. Thornton China Center Monograph Series No. 4. Washington, DC:Brookings Institution.

Liff, A. P. (2019). Unambivalent alignment: Japan's China strategy, the US Alliance, and the "hedging" fallacy. *International Relations of the Asia-Pacific*, **19**(3), 453–91.

Lim, D. J., & Mukherjee, R. (2019). Hedging in South Asia: Balancing economic and security interests amid Sino-Indian competition. *International Relations of the Asia-Pacific*, **19**(3), 493–522.

Liu, F. (2023). Balance of power, balance of alignment, and China's role in the regional order transition. *The Pacific Review*, **36** (2), 261–83. https://doi.org/10.1080/09512748.2022.2160791.

Lobell, S. E., Ripsman, N. M., & Taliaferro, J.W., eds. (2009). *Neoclassical Realism, the State, and Foreign Policy.* Cambridge: Cambridge University Press.

Macias, A. (February 7, 2021). Biden says there will be "extreme competition" with China, but won't take Trump approach. *CNBC News.* www.cnbc.com/2021/02/07/biden-will-compete-with-china-but-wont-take-trump-approach.html.

Mearsheimer, J. J. (1994/1995). The false promise of international institutions. *International Security*, **19**(3), 5–49.

Mearsheimer, J. J. (2001). *The Tragedy of Great Power Politics.* New York: WW Norton.

Mearsheimer, J. J. (2019). Bound to fail: The rise and fall of the liberal international order. *International Security*, **43**(4), 7–50.

Medeiros, E. S. (2005). Strategic hedging and the future of Asia-Pacific stability. *The Washington Quarterly*, **29**(1), 145–67.

Meibauer, G., Desmaele, L., Onea, T. et al. (2021). Rethinking neoclassical realism at theory's end. *International Studies Review*, **23**(1), 268–95.

Ministry of Defence, New Zealand (MoD). (2010). *Defence White Paper 2010.* Wellington: New Zealand Government.

Ministry of Defence, New Zealand (MoD). (2015). *Defence White Paper 2015.* Wellington: New Zealand Government.

Ministry of Defence, New Zealand (MoD). (2016). *Defence White Paper 2016*. Wellington: New Zealand Government.

Ministry of Defence, New Zealand (MoD). (2018). *Strategic Defence Policy Statement 2018*. Wellington: New Zealand Government .

Ministry of Foreign Affairs and Trade, New Zealand (MFAT). (2012). *Opening Doors to China: New Zealand's 2015 Vision*. Wellington: New Zealand Government.

Morgenthau, H. J. (1967). *Politics Among Nations: The Struggle for Power and Peace*, 4th ed. New York: Knopf.

Morrison, S. (October 3, 2019). In our interest. *Lowy Lecture*. www.pm.gov.au/media/speech-lowy-lecture-our-interest.

Morrison, S. (July 1, 2020). Address: Launch of the 2020 Defence Strategic Update. www.pm.gov.au/media/address-launch-2020-defence-strategic-update.

Murphy, A.-M. (2010). Beyond balancing and bandwagoning: Thailand's response to China's rise. *Asian Security*, **6**(1), 1–27.

Narizny, K. (2017). On systemic paradigms and domestic politics: A critique of the newest realism. *International Security*, **42**(2), 155–90.

Nye Jr., J. S. (2003). *Understanding International Conflicts: An Introduction to Theory and History*. London: Longman.

Organski, A. F. K. (1958). *World Politics*. New York: Alfred A. Knopf.

Organski, A. F. K., & Kugler, J. (1980). *The War Ledger*. Chicago: University of Chicago Press.

Pal, D., & Singh, S. V. (July 10, 2020). Multilateralism with Chinese characteristics: Bringing in the hub-and-spoke. *The Diplomat*. https://thediplomat.com/2020/07/multilateralism-with-chinese-characteristics-bringing-in-the-hub-and-spoke/.

Pape, R. A. (2005). Soft balancing against the United States. *International Security*, **30**(1), 7–45.

Park, J. J. (2011). The US-led alliances in the Asia-Pacific: Hedge against potential threats or an undesirable multilateral security order? *The Pacific Review*, **24**(2), 137–58.

Park, J. J. (2023). The US-led security network in the Indo-Pacific in international order transition: A South Korean perspective. *The Pacific Review*, **36** (2), 329–50. https://doi.org//10.1080/09512748.2022.2160790.

Paul, T. V. (2005). Soft balancing in the age of US primacy. *International Security*, **30**(1), 46–71.

Paul, T. V. (2017). Recasting statecraft: International relations and strategies of peaceful change. *International Studies Quarterly*, **61**(1), 1–13.

Paul, T. V. (2018). Assessing change in world politics. *International Studies Review*, **20**(2), 177–85.

Paul, T. V. (2021). Globalization, deglobalization and reglobalization: Adapting liberal international order. *International Affairs*, **97**(5), 1599–620.

Pugh, M. (1989). *The ANZUS Crisis, Nuclear Visiting and Deterrence.* Cambridge: Cambridge University Press.

Rachman, G. (August 17, 2020). The decoupling of the US and China has only just begun. *Financial Times*. www.ft.com/content/9000d2b0-460f-4380-b5de-cd7fdb9416c8.

Rathbun, B. (2008). A rose by any other name: Neoclassical realism as the logical and necessary extension of structural realism. *Security Studies*, **17**(2), 294–321.

Reilly, B. (2020). The return of values in Australian foreign policy. *Australian Journal of International Affairs*, **74**(2), 116–23.

Ripsman, N. M., Taliaferro, J. W., & Lobell, S. E. (2016). *Neoclassical Realist Theory of International Politics*. Oxford: Oxford University Press.

Rolland, N. (April 11, 2019). A concise guide to the Belt and Road initiative. *National Bureau of Asia Research*. www.nbr.org/publication/a-guide-to-the-belt-and-road-initiative/.

Rose, G. (1998). Neoclassical realism and theories of foreign policy. *World Politics*, **51**(1), 144–72.

Ross, R. S. (2006). Balance of power politics and the rise of China: Accommodation and balancing in East Asia. *Security Studies*, **15**(3), 355–95.

Rudd, K. (December 4, 2008). National security speech. House of Representatives, Canberra. https://parlinfo.aph.gov.au/parlInfo/genpdf/chamber/hansardr/2008-12-04/0045/hansard_frag.pdf;fileType=application%2Fpdf.

Schweller, R. L. (1994). Bandwagoning for profit: Bringing the revisionist state back in. *International Security*, **19**(1), 72–107.

Schweller, R. (1998). Deadly imbalances: Tripolarity and Hitler's strategy of world conquest. New York: Columbia University Press.

Schweller, R. L. (2003). The progressiveness of neoclassical realism. In C. Elman, & M. F. Elman, eds., *Progress in International Relations Theory: Appraising the Field*. Cambridge, MA: MIT Press, pp. 311–48.

Sil, R., & Katzenstein, P. J. (2010). Analytic eclecticism in the study of world politics: Reconfiguring problems and mechanisms across research traditions. *Perspectives on Politics*, **8**(2), 411–31.

Silver, L. (June 30, 2021). China's international image remains broadly negative as views of the U.S. rebound. Pew Research Center. www.pewresearch.org/fact-tank/2021/06/30/chinas-international-image-remains-broadly-negative-as-views-of-the-u-s-rebound/.

Smith, N. R. (2018). Can neoclassical realism become a genuine theory of international relations? *The Journal of Politics*, **80**(2), 742–49.

Steff, R., & Dodd-Parr, F. (2019). Examining the immanent dilemma of small states in the Asia-Pacific: The strategic triangle between New Zealand, the US and China. *The Pacific Review*, **32**(1), 90–112.

Stein, J. G. (2013). Threat perception in international relations. In L. Huddy, D. O. Sears, & J. S. Levy, eds., *The Oxford Handbook of Political Psychology*, 2nd ed. Oxford: Oxford University Press, pp. 364–94.

Storey, I. (2015). *Thailand's Post-Coup Relations with China and America: More Beijing, Less Washington*. Report, Trends in Southeast Asia. Singapore: ISEAS-Yusof Ishak Institute.

Storey, I. (2019). *Thailand's Military Relations with China: Moving from Strength to Strength*. Report, Perspective, No. 43. Singapore: ISEAS-Yusof Ishak Institute.

Sussangkarn, C. (2011). Chiang Mai initiative multilateralization: Origin, development, and outlook. *Asian Economic Policy Review*, **6**(2), 203–20.

Taliaferro, J. W. (2004). *Balancing Risks: Great Power Intervention in the Periphery*. Ithaca: Cornell University Press.

Tan, S. S. (2011). America the indispensable: Singapore's view of the United States' engagement in the Asia-Pacific. *Asian Affairs: An American Review*, **38**(3), 156–71.

Tan, S. S. (2016). Facilitating the US rebalance: Challenges and prospects for Singapore as America's security partner. *Security Challenges*, **12**(3), 20–33.

Tang, S. (2009). Taking stock of neoclassical realism. *International Studies Review*, **11**(4), 799–803.

Tessman, B. (2012). System structure and state strategy: Adding hedging to the menu. *Security Studies*, **21**(2), 192–231.

Tessman, B., & Wolfe, W. (2011). Great powers and strategic hedging: The case of Chinese energy security strategy. *International Studies Review*, **13**(2), 214–40.

Tow, W. T. (2019). Minilateral security's relevance to US strategy in the Indo-Pacific: Challenges and prospects. *The Pacific Review*, **32**(2), 232–44.

Turnbull, M. (March 23, 2016). Lowy lecture. www.malcolmturnbull.com.au/media/2016-lowy-lecture.

Vejjajiva, A. (September 21, 2009). Speech at a dinner talk with American trading companies. New York. www.ryt9.com/en/mfa/86566.

Walt, S. M. (1987). *The Origins of Alliance*. Ithaca: Cornell University Press.

Walton, D. (July 22, 2015). Saving America's ties with Thailand. *Wall Street Journal*. www.wsj.com/articles/saving-americas-ties-with-thailand-1437586052

Waltz, K. N. (1979). *Theory of International Politics*. Boston: Addison-Wesley.

Waltz, K. N. (1996). International politics is not foreign policy. *Security Studies*, **6**(1), 54–57.

Westcott, B. (September 18, 2021). Australia's decades-long balancing act between the US and China is over. It chose Washington. *CNN*. https://edition.cnn.com/2021/09/16/australia/australia-china-us-aukus-submarine-intl-hnk/index.html.

White House. (February, 2022a). The Indo Pacific strategy of the United States. www.whitehouse.gov/wp-content/uploads/2022/02/U.S.-Indo-Pacific-Strategy.pdf.

White House. (November 14, 2022b). Readout of the President Joe Biden's meeting with President Xi Jinping of the People's Republic of China. The White House. www.whitehouse.gov/briefing-room/statements-releases/2022/11/14/readout-of-president-joe-bidens-meeting-with-president-xi-jinping-of-the-peoples-republic-of-china/.

Wilkins, T. (2023). Middle power hedging in the era of security/economic disconnect: Australia, Japan, and the "Special Strategic Partnership." *International Relations of the Asia-Pacific*, **23**(1), 93–127.

Wohlforth, W. C. (1999). The stability of a unipolar world. *International Security*, **24**(1), 5–41.

Wohlforth, W. C. (2008). Realism. In C. Reus-Smit, & D. Snidal, eds., *The Oxford Handbook of International Relations*. Oxford: Oxford University Press, pp. 131–49.

World Economic Forum. (January 24, 2018). "The Belt and Road Impact." World Economic Forum Annual Meeting. www.weforum.org/events/world-economic-forum-annual-meeting-2018/sessions/the-belt-and-road-impact.

Yan, X. (2013). Strategic cooperation without mutual trust: A path forward for China and the United States. *Asia Policy*, **15**(1), 4–6.

Young, A. (April 19, 2021). Nanaia Mahuta likens NZ-China relations to Taniwha and Dragon. *New Zealand Herald*. www.nzherald.co.nz/nz/nanaia-mahuta-likens-nz-china-relations-to-taniwha-and-dragon/UX7W7YHM3YGT5Y634BY2TF6K4M/.

Young, J. (2017). Seeking ontological security through the rise of China: New Zealand as a small trading nation. *The Pacific Review*, **30**(4), 513–30.

Zakaria, F. (2008). *The Post-American World*. New York: WW Norton.

Authors' Bios

***Kai He** is a Professor of International Relations and the Director of the Centre for Governance and Public Policy at Griffith University in Brisbane, Australia. He is currently a non-resident Senior Scholar at the United States Institute of Peace (2022–2023). He was an Australian Research Council (ARC) Future Fellow (2017–2020) and a postdoctoral fellow in the Princeton-Harvard China and the World Program (2009–2010). He is the author of *Institutional Balancing in the Asia Pacific: Economic Interdependence and China's Rise* (Routledge, 2009) and *China's Crisis Behavior: Political Survival and Foreign Policy* (Cambridge, 2016) as well as the co-author of *Prospect Theory and Foreign Policy Analysis in the Asia Pacific: Rational Leaders and Risky Behavior* (Routledge, 2013 with Huiyun Feng) and *Contesting Revisionism: The United States, China, and Transformation of International Order* (Oxford, 2021, with Steve Chan, Huiyun Feng, and Weixing Hu).

***Huiyun Feng** is a Professor in the School of Government and International Relations at Griffith University, Australia. She is a former Jennings Randolph Peace Scholar at the United States Institute of Peace. Her publications have appeared in the *European Journal of International Relations*, *Security Studies*, *The Pacific Review*, *International Politics*, *Chinese Journal of International Politics*, and *Asian Perspective*. She is the author of *Chinese Strategic Culture and Foreign Policy Decision-Making: Confucianism, Leadership, and War* (Routledge, 2007) and the co-author of *Prospect Theory and Foreign Policy Analysis in the Asia Pacific: Rational Leaders and Risky Behavior* (Routledge, 2013) with Kai He. Her latest book is *Contesting Revisionism: The United States, China, and Transformation of International Order* (Oxford, 2021, co-authored with Steve Chan, Kai He, and Weixing Hu).

Acknowledgments

This project is supported by the Australian Research Council (DP210102843). The authors would like to thank Shaun Breslin, Rosemary Foot, Satu Limaye, John Nilsson-Wright, T. V. Paul, Rajesh Rajagopalan, Anders Wivel, as well as all the participants for their comments and suggestions at the virtual workshops on "Navigating International Order Transition in the Indo Pacific" co-sponsored by the Global Research Network on Peaceful Change (GRENPEC) and Centre for Governance and Public Policy, Griffith in September 2021. All errors and omissions are the authors' own. Kai He also acknowledges the support of the United States Institute of Peace (USIP) as a nonresident Senior Scholar in 2022–2023. The opinions, findings, and conclusions or recommendations expressed in this Element are those of the authors and do not necessarily reflect the views of the USIP.

Cambridge Elements ☰

International Relations

Series Editors

Jon C. W. Pevehouse
University of Wisconsin–Madison

Jon C. W. Pevehouse is the Mary Herman Rubinstein Professor of Political Science and Public Policy at the University of Wisconsin–Madison. He has published numerous books and articles in IR in the fields of international political economy, international organizations, foreign policy analysis, and political methodology. He is a former editor of the leading IR field journal, International Organization.

Tanja A. Börzel
Freie Universität Berlin

Tanja A. Börzel is the Professor of political science and holds the Chair for European Integration at the Otto-Suhr-Institute for Political Science, Freie Universität Berlin. She holds a PhD from the European University Institute, Florence, Italy. She is coordinator of the Research College "The Transformative Power of Europe," as well as the FP7-Collaborative Project "Maximizing the Enlargement Capacity of the European Union" and the H2020 Collaborative Project "The EU and Eastern Partnership Countries: An Inside-Out Analysis and Strategic Assessment." She directs the Jean Monnet Center of Excellence "Europe and its Citizens."

Edward D. Mansfield
University of Pennsylvania

Edward D. Mansfield is the Hum Rosen Professor of Political Science, University of Pennsylvania. He has published well over 100 books and articles in the area of international political economy, international security, and international organizations. He is Director of the Christopher H. Browne Center for International Politics at the University of Pennsylvania and former program co-chair of the American Political Science Association.

Editorial Team

International Relations Theory
Jeffrey T. Checkel, European University Institute, Florence

International Political Economy
Edward D. Mansfield, University of Pennsylvania

Stafanie Walter, University of Zurich

International Security
Sarah Kreps, Cornell University

Anna Leander, Graduate Institute Geneva

International Organisations
Tanja A. Börzel, Freie Universität Berlin

Jon C. W. Pevehouse, University of Wisconsin–Madison

About the Series

The Cambridge Elements Series in International Relations
publishes original research on key topics in the field. The series includes
manuscripts addressing international security, international political economy,
international organizations, and international relations.

Cambridge Elements ≡

International Relations

Elements in the Series

Social Media and International Relations
Sarah Kreps

Across Type, Time and Space: American Grand Strategy inComparative Perspective
Peter Dombrowski and Simon Reich

Moral Psychology, Neuroscience, and International Norms
Richard Price and Kathryn Sikkink

Contestations of the Liberal International Order
Fredrik Söderbaum, Kilian Spandler, Agnese Pacciardi

Domestic Interests, Democracy, and Foreign Policy Change
Brett Ashley Leeds, Michaela Mattes

Token Forces: How Tiny Troop Deployments Became Ubiquitous in UN Peacekeeping
Katharina P. Coleman, Xiaojun Li

The Dual Nature of Multilateral Development Banks
Laura Francesca Peitz

Peace in Digital International Relations
Oliver P. Richmond, Gëzim Visoka, Ioannis Tellidis

Regionalized Governance in the Global South
Brooke Coe, Kathryn Nash

Digital Globalization
Stephen Weymouth

The Local Political Economy of IMF Lending: Partisanship, Protection, Punishment, and Protest
Rodwan Abouharb, Bernhard Reinsberg

After Hedging: Hard Choices for the Indo-Pacific States between the United States and China
Kai He, Huiyun Feng

A full series listing is available at: www.cambridge.org/EIR

Printed in the United States
by Baker & Taylor Publisher Services